Festive Crafts

Mary Ann Green

Frederick Muller Limited
London

Throughout this book, measurements are supplied in metric and imperial figures. The two sets of figures are not always exact equivalents, so follow one set of measurements only.

Acknowledgements

The prints on pages 20, 66 and 90 are published with thanks to the Mary Evans Picture Library. The picture opposite page 1 is published with thanks to the BBC Hulton Picture Library. Thanks are also due to W.I. Publications Ltd. for allowing us to use their instructions for the making of the Harvest Maid from their publication on Corn Dollies. Photography by Chris Sowe and Brian Bottomley. Large artwork by Michael Green. Working drawings by the author. Illustrations on pages 32 and 33 by Denis Hawkins. Thanks are also due to Lynne Isaacs, Joan Rendell, Judy Walker, Frank Davies and Gunvor Selkirk for their help.

First published in Great Britain in 1983 by Frederick Muller Limited, Dataday House, Alexandra Road, London SW19 7JZ.

Copyright © 1983 Mary Ann Green

British Library Cataloguing in Publication Data
Green, Mary Ann
    Festive crafts.
    1. Handicrafts – Great Britain
    I. Title
    680   TT57

ISBN 0 584 11035 9

Printed in Italy

Contents

Christmas in Alsace. In southern Germany Frau Berchta, goddess of light, makes her appearance on January 6th, leading her band of good and evil spirits. Her day coincides with the Christian Feast of the Epiphany and is celebrated by the offering of meals.

CANDLEMAKING

Apart from its religious significance, the lighted candle is inseparably linked with the old pagan fire festivals of Europe. Within the church, candles were lit in celebration of purity and new life. Even among the ancient peoples and long before the spread of Christianity, they were associated with a ritualistic cleansing by light and fire. Whether a flaming brand taken from the festal fire, or a simple wax candle, they drove away evil and purified by their very presence.

Both Druids and Norsemen lit fires at the winter solstice to drive out evil demons and welcome the return of the sun. The domestic counterpart of these fires has survived in the form of the Yule Log which is still burned in parts of Europe. A quaint remnant of this ritual was recorded in Penryn in Cornwall in 1884, where a children's Christmas game of dancing round the candles was still in vogue at that time. A basket filled with sand and stuck with lighted candles was placed on the floor and singing and dancing performed in circles round it, a vestige of these ancient fire rites.

So many of the religious festivals celebrated over the Christmas season have their roots in the pre-Christian festivals of light and fire which welcomed the winter solstice. Although banned by the early church as a heathen practice, the burning of candles in church and home at Christmas was re-established and eventually became a significant part of the celebrations.

During the Jewish Hannukah, candles are lit on each of the eight days of the festival. They commemorate the rededication of the temple after it was cleansed of pagan influence and restored for Jewish worship. Symbolically, the lighted candle represents to all religions the continuance of the light of faith.

The first day of February, a quarter day in the natural

pastoral calendar, saw the beginning of spring lambing on most farms. Once again the old merged with the new and the Celtic lambing festival became incorporated with the Christian celebration of Candlemas Day on February 2nd. This day commemorates with the blessing of candles, the presentation of Christ in the temple and the purification of the Virgin Mary. It is thought to derive from the pagan Feast of Lights and in part from the Roman Lupercalia, which was held in mid-February and dedicated to Pluto, god of the underworld. Both festivals featured candle-lit displays and the early Christians merely tailored these ancient celebrations to fit their own beliefs, dedicating the February feast anew and decreeing that the candles be lit in honour of the Virgin Mary and Holy Child. During the service parishioners received their consecrated candles with thanks. They believed them to have curative powers and when relighted they would protect against ill fortune and the devil.

The "churching" of women after childbirth also took place at Candlemas and it became customary for young mothers to carry lighted tapers on their first day of worship following the birth. Signs of purity are seen in the garden at this time as the snowdrop, the Fair Maid of February, pushes up through the soil.

Most of the Catholic countries hold Easter Eve, the Saturday before Easter Sunday, as a fire festival. Hundreds of candles are lit from a great bonfire outside the church in a celebration of the new fire of Easter Night. Effigies of Judas are still burned on the two days preceding Easter in places as far apart as Greece and Latin America. Even the South End of Liverpool celebrates Good Friday in this way. The thin veneer of Christianity suggests the new fire as symbolic of Christ and the effigy as Judas Iscariot, but there is little doubt that the customs are pagan in origin.

In England, the hallowed paschal candle which dates from the third century AD, is the most important of the Christian year. Three feet tall and cast in pure beeswax, it is marked with the sign of the Cross, the first and last letters of the Greek alphabet and the year, hence the number of years of redemption. Sealed inside are five grains of incense, representing the five wounds of Christ. Traditionally lit outside the church, it is carried in procession into the darkened building and placed by the font, where it burns until Ascension Day. After that it is relit for each baptism and a fresh light taken from it for each child baptised. In country places the wax was endowed with special powers and was dripped at crucial points about the house and farm to ward off witches!

Our ancestors, Protestant and Catholic alike, were prey to the omens and superstitions attached to candles. They used them to predict fortune, good and bad, and lit them at births, deaths and marriages to keep evil spirits at bay. In the autumn, as the souls in purgatory were released on All Hallow's Eve, they featured in ghostly hill-top processions in a few northern counties. On many farms the candles were kept burning all night, along with the Hallow fires which were lit at dusk, to keep home and stock from harm. These beliefs were reflected in the place names – Purgatory Field and Purgatory Farm, both recorded in Lancashire about eighty years ago.

Sweden has its own patron Saint of Light, St Lucia, whose feast day on December 13th heralds the start of the Christmas season. Each town elects a pretty blonde Lucia queen, who visits the houses well before dawn, dressed in white and wearing a crown of woven bilberry twigs and flickering candles. Her white dress and red sash represent light and fire, her visit carrying a promise of longer days and a new year of plenty. It is worth noting that before the Gregorian reform of the calendar, her visit fell on the shortest day of the year. More recently it has become the custom to hold the celebrations within the family. The youngest daughter of the house, wearing the crown, wakes her parents at first light with a breakfast of coffee and saffron coloured Lucia buns.

St Lucia, who was martyred for her Christian beliefs, was

originally from Sicily and it was only by a coincidence of dates that she was embraced by the Christian festival. In Italy her day is still kept as a festival of fire.

The wax from the Yule Candle, once the splendid centre-piece of the Christmas table, was thought to have magical powers. The stub end was cherished and put aside on Twelfth Night to be relit during thunder-storms to prevent the house being rent by lightning. In Sweden, at the start of the spring ploughing, the farmer would smear the plough blades with tallow from the Yule Candle, to bless the soil and ensure fertility for the coming year. In England he offered his prayers in church on Plough Sunday, the first Sunday after Twelfth Night. A plough was taken before the altar and blessed and a candle lit in a plea for abundant crops. Candles were expensive, and in the Middle Ages farm workers collected alms for the "plough light" which was kept burning in the church throughout the year. Although work in the fields was supposed to start on Plough Monday, the day was given over to celebration as the Plough Stots and sword dancers travelled the parish dragging with them the beribboned "Fool Plough" and asking for largesse.

Universally, candles and lanterns light the home at Christmas. Even the dead are not forgotten in the darkest parts of northern Europe where their graves are decorated with lights. A candle in the window traditionally lit the way for the Holy Family to Bethlehem. Today it symbolises hopes for a year of light, warmth and plenty.

BASIC CANDLEMAKING MATERIAL

When candlemaking was exclusively a domestic art, candles were made from a variety of waxes gleaned from both animal and vegetable sources. Ordinary household tapers were made of tallow (rendered down animal fat) which gave off a great deal of smoke and had a revolting smell. The alternative, beeswax, burned clear and bright with little smoke and gave a gentle perfume of honey, but it was scarce and consequently expensive. Some country people, particularly settlers in the New World, also used fat extracted from berries. These were picked in the early winter after the first heavy frosts, mainly from the various species of myrtle, and scalded in boiling water. The wax was collected as it floated to the surface. After being rendered down and sieved a few times to remove impurities, it was moulded into small candles which burned with a spicy perfume. Today we use paraffin wax, a by-product of petrol.

Paraffin wax

Ranging from white to cream in colour, this can be bought refined and in granulated form. The average melting temperature is 56–58°C (133–136°F), although there are different grades available with higher and lower melting temperatures.

Stearin (stearic acid)

A necessary additive for hardening the paraffin wax. It acts as a good solvent for dye, aids release from the mould and produces a longer burning candle. Use 10% stearin to wax.

Wax dyes

These can be bought in solid or powder form. In an emergency coloured wax crayons may be used, but the colour they produce is rather dull.

Wicks

These are made from plaited cotton and are available in several thicknesses to suit the diameter of the candle. It is very important to use the correct size of wick. If the wick is too thick, the candle will smoke; if too thin it will be extinguished by flooding. Most commercial moulds are sold with the correct size wick but if you want the candle to leave a hollow wax shell as it burns, use a slightly smaller size wick than usual.

Oil-soluble perfume

The use of scented candles can be traced back to classical Rome where the first Christian Emperor, Constantine the Great, made provision for scented wax candles to be burned in church. The paraffin wax we use today is odourless so we add essential oils to provide perfume. The choice is wide, ranging from sweet and delicate to musky. My own favourites are lemon and jasmine. The perfume is added to the hot wax just before it is poured into the mould to prevent the ingredients from evaporating. Alternatively, you can soak the wick in perfume before fixing it in the mould.

EQUIPMENT

Moulds

A silicone rubber mould will give fine relief, while metal and plastic moulds give a sharper, more polished finish. Many of the gimmicky, chunky candle shapes often do not burn well and a plain mould will give you a beautifully coloured candle which will burn evenly without smoking. You can always decorate the surface or add a perfume if the candle is to be used for a special occasion.

Improvised moulds

These can be made from a variety of discarded household containers – plastic detergent and shampoo bottles, yoghurt pots, milk and cottage cheese cartons, straight-sided mugs and cups made redundant by the loss of a handle. Rolled cones of embossed wallpaper make interesting texture moulds and for round candles you can use rubber balls. Any container with surface decoration or one that is narrower at the top than the bottom, can only be used once as the candle will have to be cut out. Free-form shapes can be cast by pouring wax into pieces of crinkled-up kitchen foil.

Make a hole for the wick in the centre of the base, using a skewer heated over a flame. If the mould is pottery or glass, the bottom of the wick can be weighted down by a wick sustainer or a small metal washer and the wax poured in the usual way. It is best to lightly oil the inside of any home-made mould before pouring in the wax.

Double boiler

If you do not have a double boiler, you can substitute two old saucepans, one inside the other. *Never heat wax directly over an open flame.* Use an asbestos mat as an added precaution over a gas flame.

Mould seal

Use mould seal or Plasticine to prevent leakage round the wick.

Wicking needle

This is only necessary if you are using a flexible rubber mould which could get damaged at its weakest point, round the wick hole.

Thermometer

Use a sugar thermometer, not a room or body thermometer. This is essential for successful candlemaking.

Perfumed Christmas Candle (a basic moulded candle)

Common features of the Christmas festivities are the Yule Log and the Yule Candle, which were both lit at the same time on Christmas Eve. The fire was not allowed to go out until the Log was burnt to ashes and the Candle remained alight throughout the Christmas Eve supper. It was then relit by the head of the household on each successive evening of the twelve days of Christmas, to be finally extinguished on Twelfth Night. The unburnt end was thought to have great protective powers and was lovingly put away for the next year and held as a charm against evil.

The original Yule Candle once seen in Great Britain, Ireland and the Scandinavian countries, was large and ornate, often coloured and decorated with sprigs of evergreen. In America, the early settlers experimented with waxes and perfumes extracted from plants. During the 1700s, the burning of bayberry candles at Christmas was as traditional as the burning of the Yule Log in Europe. These fragrant candles were made from wax taken from the precious berries of the *Myrica pensylvanica*, one of the myrtle family, and were still being made in North Carolina a few years ago. To the American colonials the bayberry candles were so prized that a fine was levied on anyone found picking the berries before the autumn.

You will need:

A cylindrical mould approx. 10 cm (4 in) high and 6 cm (2¼ in) diameter
20 tbsps granulated paraffin wax
2 tbsps stearin
⅛ dye disc, red
Approx. 20 cm (8 in) length of 5 cm (2 in) wicking

Oil-based perfume (optional) – use bayberry for Christmas
Mould seal or Plasticine. Sugar thermometer. Double boiler.

To make:

Using the double boiler, slowly melt the paraffin wax to a
temperature of 82°C (180°F). Knot one end of the wick. Dip
the whole wick in hot wax and pull straight while it is still
warm and pliable. Thread through the base of the mould and
seal over the knot with Plasticine on the outside. Pull taut and
tie the free end to a skewer or pencil placed centrally across
the top of the mould. (*Diag. 1.*) Tie as tightly as possible to
prevent the wick wilting when the hot wax is poured.

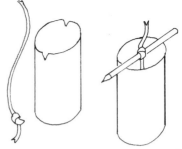

*Diag. 1. Knot the wick onto a pencil
or a skewer.*

Using a separate container and double boiler, dissolve the
dye in stearin. When completely dissolved, add to the melted
wax and reheat to 82°C (180°F). If perfume is to be used, add
to the wax now, following the supplier's instructions. Pour
the wax into the centre of the mould (*Diag. 2.*) until it reaches
1 cm (½ in) from the top, reserving a little wax for topping up.
Let the wax stand for a few minutes, then tap the sides of the
mould gently to release any air bubbles. If rapid cooling and
therefore a smooth finish is required, stand the mould in a
bath of cold water, so that the water level is the same as the
level of the wax, and weight the mould to hold it down.

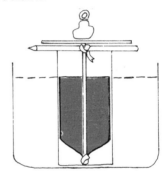

Diag. 2. Pour the wax into the mould.

After 15 minutes, check to see if a well has appeared round
the wick. Break the surface skin of the wax with a skewer and
top up round the wick (*Diag. 3.*) with the remaining wax
reheated to temperature. Take care not to overfill when
topping up or the wax will run to the sides and form a wedge
between the mould and the candle (*Diag. 4.*), making it
difficult to remove. Return it to the cold water bath to harden.
The topping up process may need to be repeated.

When the candle has finally cooled over a period of several
hours, remove the mould seal. Turn it upside down and tap
gently so that the candle slides out. If it is difficult to remove

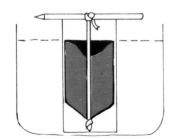

Diag. 3. Top up round the wick.

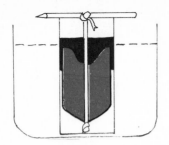

Diag. 4. *Do not overfill.*

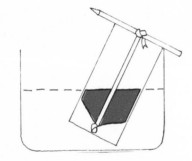

Diag. 5. *Prop the mould at an angle.*

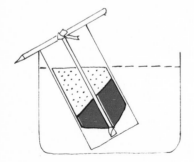

Diag. 6. *Making a candle with diagonal stripes.*

stand in the refrigerator for half an hour and repeat. Trim the wick and level the base of the candle.

To decorate make a small garland of evergreens and berries to encircle the base, or try shaping some leaves by hand out of warm wax.

DECORATIVE EFFECTS

Striped Candles

Prepare the mould and wick as described on page 9. Select the number of colours required. If you want the stripes to be even, mark the mould on the inside before pouring the wax. Heat the first colour of wax to 82°C (180°F) and pour into the mould. Allow to cool until rubbery, using a cooling bath if you have one. If the wax is allowed to get too hard, the layers will not fuse together; if it is too soft, the hot wax will melt the lower layer, mixing the colours.

Heat the second colour to 82°C (180°F) and pour into the mould. You can build the candle up gradually in as many different coloured stripes as desired. Finally, top up the wax round the wick as before. If the stripes are quite deep, each layer of colour may need to be topped up separately.

Diagonal Stripes

Prop the mould at alternate angles while pouring and cooling the wax for each colour. (*Diags. 5 & 6.*)

Textured Candles

The all-over stippled effect created by hammering looks best on a plain-shaped and single-coloured candle. It is done while the wax is still quite soft, during the cooling stage. Working from the bottom to the top and turning it as you go, tap the candle with a small, ball-ended tack hammer. The outer surface will bruise and look lighter than the untouched wax.

Indentations can be made with small objects, such as the hexagonal end of a pencil, and the hollows accentuated with coloured poster paint. Leaves and berries can be cut from a sheet of wax and welded to the surface of the candle with a hot knife.

When the inevitable mistakes occur, render down the wax and turn it to good use by casting a decorative moulded candle with the maximum amount of relief. Highlight the dull brown colour with gold paint to give an "antique" effect.

Rubber Moulded Candle

For a rubber mould, prepare and fix the correct size wick, then suspend the mould between two fixed battens, making an improvised rack. Do not support it in a box which would prevent the air circulating, or in a water bath where the pressure of water might cause distortion. Use only 1% stearin to wax and add when dissolving the dye. Heat the wax to the recommended temperature for each type of mould.

Pour the wax into the mould and leave until absolutely cold before removing, or some of the surface detail may get damaged. To remove, rub the surface of the mould with soapy hands and peel off carefully. Wash and dry and store well away from heat and sunlight. Buff up the matt surface of the candle with a soft cloth. (A small amount of beeswax in the candle mixture will make this easier.)

Dipped Tapers

Dipping is the oldest method of candlemaking, the way the old tallow tapers were made. The length of the cigar-shaped candle is governed by the size of the container used to hold the melted wax. Ideally tapers are made in pairs, but it is best to experiment with a single one to begin with until you are familiar with the method.

You will need:

Paraffin wax, sufficient to fill the chosen container
Wax dye
38 cm (15 in) narrow wicking (double if making a pair)
A deep metal container for the wax (try a catering size instant coffee tin)
Length of wooden dowelling, approx. 1 cm (⅜ in) diameter, or a wooden coat hanger
Sugar thermometer, handicraft knife

To make:

Prepare the paraffin wax with dye and stearin as described on page 9, and heat to 82°C (180°F), standing the metal container in a saucepan of water for safety. Tie one end of the wicking securely round the wooden rod. Dip the wick in hot wax, remove and pull straight while still warm and pliable. Lower the wick slowly and evenly into the wax, hold for a few seconds then lift out and leave to dry for a minute before repeating the process. In between dips, rest the rod across the back of two chairs and catch the drips of wax on a newspaper. Repeat the process until the taper is the desired thickness, then hang it up to dry and harden completely for a couple of hours. Cut the taper off the rod and even up the base, using the handicraft knife. Finally, trim the wick.

To give the candle a shiny finish, bring the heat of the wax up to 93°C (200°F) for the final dip, then dip the taper in cold water, making sure the wick does not get wet.

Floating Candles

The Greeks believed that candles symbolised life and that the number of candles displayed at a birthday feast represented

the number of years lived. Good luck will follow if all the flames can be blown out with one breath and if a wish is made, but not spoken, it will come true.

Floating candles are very simple to make and look pretty as a table centrepiece for a child's birthday party.

You will need:

4 large walnuts
32 cm (12 in) narrow wicking
Paraffin wax
Impact adhesive, sharp handicraft knife

To make:

Using the handicraft knife, carefully halve the walnuts and remove the contents of each shell. Heat the wax to 82°C (180°F). Cut the wicking into eight 4 cm (1½ in) lengths. Knot one end then dip in wax and pull straight. Place a blob of impact adhesive centrally in the base of each nutshell and push the knotted end of the wicks on top, with the help of a matchstick, so that the wicks stand up vertically. Stand the shells in an old egg box and leave the glue to dry. Fill the shells with wax. Allow it to set, then top up round the wick.

Float the walnut shells in a shallow dish of water.

Floating star shaped candles can be made for the Christmas table by using *small* biscuit or pastry cutters as moulds. Oil the cutters and press into a flat bed of Plasticine or self-hardening modelling clay smeared with oil, to prevent the wax leaking. Attach the wicks to metal wick sustainers. Dip completely in hot wax and pull straight. Position in centre of mould and pour wax as above. When set remove from mould and leave overnight to harden.

Paper Candle Ring

In Denmark it is still customary to light the Christmas tree with real candles, usually red or white. The same colour

Diag. 7.   Trace the flower shapes.

Diag. 8.   Trace the leaf shapes.

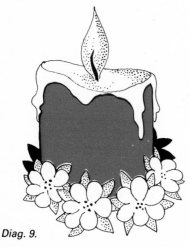

Diag. 9.

scheme is used for the dining table and the larger candles are always decorated with candle rings made from sprigs of evergreen twisted together, ribbon or cut out paper shapes.

This candle ring will fit the Christmas candle on page 8. Make it from brightly glossed heavyweight paper or from green and gold foil board (see list of suppliers).

You will need:

Scraps of stiff paper in dark green and red
Glue, tracing paper, sharp scissors, compass and pencil, card

To make:

Using your compass, draw a circle 8 cm (3¼ in) in diameter on green paper. Draw a second circle 7 cm (2¼ in) in diameter inside the first one. Cut out the ring using sharp scissors. Trace the leaf shape from *Diag. 8.* and transfer to card. Cut out and use as a template.

Cut ten leaf shapes from the green paper. Make a crease at the base of each sepal by bending up against the thumb nail. Trace the flower from *Diag. 7.* and make a template as before. Cut ten flower shapes from red paper. Snip carefully between each petal along the lines marked. Bend each petal up as described for the leaves.

Glue the leaves to the circular base, spacing evenly. When dry, glue the flowers inside the leaves. Mark the stamens with a felt tip pen or glue four or five tiny beads in place. (*Diag. 9.*)

A Wreath of Lights

Symbolic in design and very much part of the Scandinavian tradition of celebrating the winter solstice with a blaze of lights, are the candle wreaths modelled from Troll's dough or salt dough. The wreath represents the full circle of the completed year and bears the lighted candles of continuing

A wreath of lights, symbolically the flame of continuing life.

life. A wreath of candles can look welcoming flickering in the window on Christmas Eve or as part of the festive table.

You will need:

600 g (1 lb 4 oz) plain white flour
150 g (5 oz) salt
Water for mixing
Kitchen foil
6 red or white candles, 2 cm (¾ in) in diameter

To make:

Pre-heat the oven to 93°C, 200°F, gas mark ¼.
Cover a baking sheet in kitchen foil and mark a circle in the centre approximately 15 cm (6 in) in diameter, by drawing round a saucer.

Sieve the flour and salt together. Mix with water making a firm, smooth dough which is not sticky and is easy to handle. Set aside approximately one quarter of the dough for the decorations and the centre struts. Roll the remaining dough into a long rope approximately 5 cm (2 in) in diameter. Place on the baking sheet, laying it round the edge of the circle marked on the foil. Moisten the ends with water and press together to join into a circle. Smooth over the join to make even.

Roll out 6 ropes of dough roughly 1.5 cm (½ in) thick and make into two plaits about 15 cm (6 in) in length. Lay in the centre of the wreath to make a cross. Moisten the ends with water and join to the underside of the circular base.

Make six marks on the top of the base, spaced evenly round the circle where you intend the candles to stand. Using one of the candles as a tool, make a hole with the flat end of the candle, pressing it straight down into the dough. Make sure that the sides of the holes are absolutely vertical so that the candles will burn evenly when lit. Remove the candle from the wreath.

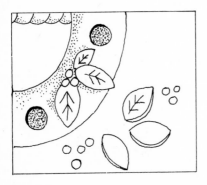

Diag. 10.　Arrange the leaves all round the wreath.

To add surface decoration, roll out the remaining dough quite thinly and using a sharp knife, cut out several leaf shapes. Mark the veins on the surface. Arrange on the wreath, moistening the undersides with water to join. Group the leaves in twos and threes round the candle holes. Roll tiny balls of dough to make berries and secure in position by pressing them to the wreath with a knitting needle through the centre. Flowers can be made and added in the same way. (*Diag. 10.*) If extra dough is needed for the decoration, mix up a small amount using one part of salt to three parts of plain flour.

Bake overnight in a slow oven. When cool, trim the foil away so there is just enough for the wreath to sit on. Should the candle holes distort during the baking, shave a little off the base of each candle with a sharp knife.

Pretty alternatives are small, individual wreaths, each one with a candle in the centre.

LANTERNS

In Sweden they call the uncovered flame the "living light". You can make these lanterns from thick metal foil and stand them along the window sill at Christmas. The pattern is pricked out with a knitting needle and is reminiscent of traditional Mexican tin work.

Open Lantern

You will need:

17 cm × 25 cm (6½ in × 10 in) heavyweight gold foil, available from craft shops
1 polystyrene tile
2 knitting needles, one large, one fine
Metal lid approx. 10 cm (4 in) in diameter to stand candle on
Impact adhesive, greaseproof paper, compass

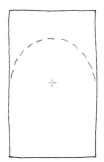

Diag. 11.   Cut along the drawn line.

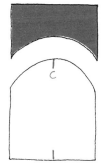

Diag. 12.   Mark centre top and bottom.

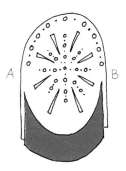

Diag. 13.   Glue the two sections together.

Diag. 14. Cut the slashes with a handicraft knife.

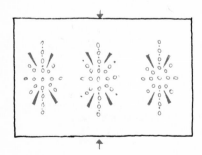

Diag. 15. Punch out the pattern three times.

To make:

Cut the foil to size and mark the centre. Using your compass draw a half circle 16.5 cm (6½ in) in diameter on the top half of the rectangle. Cut along the line. (*Diag. 11.*) The off cut will become the front of the lantern. (*Diag. 12.*)

Trace the pattern from *Diag. 14.* onto greaseproof paper. Lay the foil on top of the tile and mark the centre top. Position the tracing on top of the foil, matching centres and 2.5 cm (1 in) from the top edge. Secure with Sellotape.

Using both knitting needles, carefully punch out the pattern through both paper and foil. Punch a line of holes, alternating large and small, round the top edge of the lantern, between points A and B. (*Diag. 13.*)

Join the front and back sections of the lantern with impact adhesive, tucking the side edges of the front into the back. Stand a lighted candle in the tin lid and place the lantern over the top.

Cylindrical Lantern

You will need:

Heavyweight silver foil, 17 cm × 30 cm (6½ in × 12 in). If difficult to get, use the bottoms of large frozen food containers.
Equipment as above

To make:

Cut the foil to size and mark the centre of each long edge. Lay on the tile. Make a tracing of the pattern in *Diag. 14.* and position over the foil, matching centres. Punch out the design as previously described. Using the same tracing, repeat twice more, making one pattern on either side of the centre one. (*Diag. 15.*) Roll the foil into a cylinder (this can be done round a tin) and join the edges with impact adhesive.

A more sturdy alternative which can be used out of doors, can be made from any tin can, size and shape immaterial. *(Diag. 16.)* Remove the label and open and clean the tin. Mark the pattern on the metal using a felt tip pen. Punch the holes using a large nail and a hammer. Place a block of wood inside the tin to act as a support. Ideally this should be held in a vice while working.

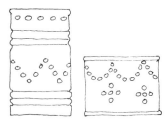

Diag. 16. Tin can lanterns.

Orange Peel Lantern

These are very quick to make and look most effective grouped together in twos or threes on the Christmas table or round the tree. They also make attractive patio lights for a summer evening party. Choose thick skinned oranges that are easy to peel.

You will need:

Oranges
Narrow wicking
Wick sustainers or small metal washers
Vegetable cooking oil

To make:

Cut each orange horizontally into two halves. Scoop out the flesh using a spoon, being careful not to damage the peel. Using kitchen scissors or a sharp, pointed knife, cut a circle 2.5 cm (1 in) in diameter from the centre of one half. *(Diag. 17.)* Cut a 5 cm (2 in) length of wicking, knot one end and pull through the wick sustainer. Position in the centre of the bottom half of the orange and half fill with vegetable oil. Light the wick and place the top cover in position.

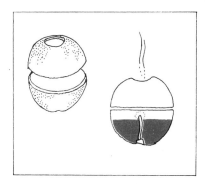

Diag. 17. Put vegetable oil in the bottom half of the orange.

Raising the Maypole in an English village.

WREATHS AND GARLANDS

The worship of plants and trees extends back to the pre-agricultural phase of man's history, when most of Europe was covered with huge, primeval forests. To early man, the tree was symbolic of life itself and, after shedding its leaves in autumn, came to represent a rebirth with the unfurling of the buds in spring. Likewise, during the cold winter months, when most plants had died or lay dormant underground, the shiny evergreen was thought to be a sign of undying life. This image of the Tree of Life is present in most civilizations, the trunk, rooted in darkness, linking Heaven and Earth with its life-giving sap.

Almost every culture had a sacred tree which embodied in its seasonal changes the renewal of life from a sacred source. Throughout Africa, sap-filled trees were thought to be the embodiment of divine motherhood. The Scandinavians held sacred the rowan or mountain ash and in Norse mythology it was named *Yggdrasil*, the World Tree. The theme of sacred life manifesting itself in the form of light and fire also runs through religion and mythology and parallel to this runs the image of the burning tree or bush.

In anticipation of the arrival of spring, the Romans named the month of April *Asperice*. It signified the opening of the earth to receive seed and it is throughout this month that we see the stirrings of life following the long, cold winter.

During the bleak weeks of Lent, Swedish children go out and cut birch twigs to decorate the home. They bind them with brightly dyed chicken feathers and as the first buds break in the warmth of the house, the first day of spring is welcomed. Apart from its association in northern Europe with the return of spring, in England the birch tree was thought to have the power to avert evil. For this purpose it was quite common to see protective branches hung on the door lintel or a few sprigs worn as a buttonhole. Although not recognised by the church, for a couple to "jump over a besom" was once considered as good as being married.

English villagers celebrated the new season on Easter Day when they bedecked their houses with white and gold garlands of flowers; yellow daffodils and primroses, sweet white violets, furry catkins and branches of pussy-willow, the Easter Palm carried to church on Palm Sunday.

This period of growth and increase on the land is celebrated in most countries on May Day and its preceding eve. The pre-Christian festival associated with it was the feast of Beltane, which marked an old Celtic quarter day when dawn bonfires were lit in the fields to drive out evil demons and thus make the land safe for the return of livestock. Lighting fires of celebration has survived in Sweden where it is done on Walpurgis Eve, the spirit of the fire symbolising the coming of the sun. Of course the people of southern Europe don't truly understand the huge relief felt by those in the north as the days lengthen and the long, dark nights come to an end.

The spirit of summer vegetation is rarely absent from the May parades. Wreathed in oak and hawthorn leaves he takes many forms; Jack-in-the-Green, the Wild Man, Green George. His counterparts exist throughout Europe. In parts of Germany he is accompanied by a man dressed in straw, a symbol of winter left behind.

At the winter solstice, the evergreen, glossy symbol of eternal life, was always used for decoration. It flourished and bore fruit when all other plants had died and was used in sacred rites to ensure the return of vegetation. Shrines of evergreen branches were built by the Druids so that the spirits of the wood could shelter and take refuge until the milder days of spring. Roman temples dedicated to their gods were festooned with laurel for the December Saturnalia and in recognition of victory the Greeks placed crowns of laurel on the heads of all their great men.

The laurel bush has always been held in high regard and was eventually adopted by the Christians as an acceptable decoration for both home and church. In 604 St Augustine of Canterbury was given permission by Pope Gregory I to use evergreens at Christmas time. Today the Americans fashion their Christmas wreaths from laurel and bay, a direct link with the customs of ancient Rome.

Most houses in England include holly and mistletoe in their decorations at Christmas, although ivy, rosemary and branches of fir are seen too. There is a superstition that they must not be brought into the house before Christmas Eve and then are to be taken down and burnt on January 6th, Twelfth Night.

Although the holly bush was revered before it was adopted by the Christians, it was said to have foretold the crucifixion. The prickly leaves warned of the crown of thorns and the red berries represented the blood of Christ. It also collected attendant superstitions and was thought to be a strong repellant against witches, demons and the Evil Eye! The prickly leaved variety was traditionally male and consequently lucky for man, the smooth leaved, variegated holly was thought to be a female luck token. Dreams of a future mate could be ensured if the lady in question gathered nine female holly leaves on a Friday, and knotted them in her three-cornered hankie at midnight. On a more practical note, wood from the holly tree will always burn cheerily when all other logs are sodden through.

Mistletoe, the Golden Bough of classical legend, featured strongly in the religions of both Druids and Norsemen. In the Celtic religion, it was held doubly sacred if found growing on an oak and the soul of the tree was thought to be present in the mistletoe. It was cut with ceremonial flourish by a high priest of the cult, using a golden sickle and caught in the white robes of another as it fell, for the plant must never touch the ground.

In Norse mythology it was Balder the Beautiful, the young sun god who was slain by a mistletoe dart put in the hand of the blind Hoder, by the evil Loki. The other gods were angry and brought Balder back to life, making the mistletoe plant swear that it would never harm another soul, mortal or immortal.

Many farms in England kept a ball of hawthorn and mistletoe hanging in the kitchen throughout the year. First thing on New Year's morning it was carried to the first sown wheat field and burnt and the ashes scattered over the soil. The bush was symbolic of the crown of thorns and the burning a purification ceremony.

Although known as a plant of peace, mistletoe is the only one of the evergreens unable to shake off its pagan associations and consequently it is not allowed inside a church. The one odd exception being the branch which is presented annually at Christmas at the high altar of York Minster.

Rosemary has long been a magical plant and was formerly included with the other decorations at Christmas time. An old legend tells of Mary hanging the baby Jesus's clothes on a rosemary bush to dry, during their long flight to Egypt. The leaves imparted sweetness to the clothes and were therefore blessed by God. Gradually abandoned as a decoration, it is now used for culinary and medicinal purposes and is one of the cure-all herbs of the herbalist as it can be applied externally to an open wound or taken as a drink.

And so as we garland our houses with evergreens and flowers for Christmas or May Day we are keeping alive the relics of ancient tree worship held sacred by our ancestors.

Evergreen Wreath

The custom of "going-a-gooding" on St Thomas's Day, December 21st, was still being practised in some parts of

England forty years ago, although by that time it was done more to honour the tradition and keep it alive, than to ask for alms. Originally the practice was confined to women and children, especially widows, who walked from house to house collecting corn and milk for baking the Christmas loaf. In Midland villages they often carried a gossiping pot and begged for frumenty. In return, they offered bunches of holly and mistletoe which were hung on the front door to show that the occupants were mindful of the Christmas spirit and had given to the poor. These lucky sprigs were the forerunners of the Christmas bunches which we still see today.

The evergreen wreath for the door is a much later innovation and came to England via America and the Scandinavian immigrants.

You will need:

Thick galvanized wire (or use a 30 cm (12 in) diameter wreath
    frame available from florists)
Fine florists wire
1 packet florists stub wires
Sphagnum moss
Sprays of evergreen; the traditional ones are bay, rosemary,
    ivy, holly and mistletoe
Small larch cones and red berries for decoration
Secateurs. Red ribbon

To make:

Drench all the evergreens with water as soon as possible after picking to clean the leaves, then stand with the bruised ends in water overnight before working.

Cut the galvanized wire into four lengths of 102 cm (40 in). Make each length into a circle 30 cm (12 in) in diameter, twisting the cut ends round each other to secure. Bind the four circles together using florists wire. Pad all round with dampened moss *(Diag. 1.)* bound securely with wire. Try not

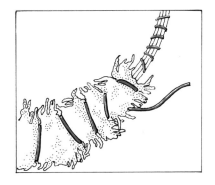

Diag. 1. Pad all round with dampened moss.

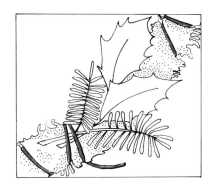

Diag. 2. Overlap each group of leaves.

Diag. 3. Wire each group individually.

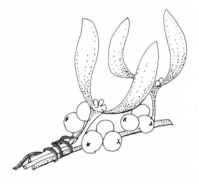

Diag. 4.

to attach the moss in lumps but tease it out gently before wiring and pad to a firm thickness of 5 cm (2 in).

Separate all the foliage into small sprays and trim the stalks to approximately 10 cm (4 in). Keep back any sprigs of mistletoe, fir cones and groups of berries to be attached later. Keep the wreath damp as you work and remember that the back surface remains flat and undecorated.

Using lengths of florists wire, bind the sprays of greenery by the stalks to the moss covered base. Lay them in one direction *(Diag. 2.)* and overlap each group of leaves slightly as you work round the circle. Using the stub wires attach each group of cones or berries individually. *(Diags. 3 & 4.)* Trim the stalks to 5 cm (2 in) and bind each one tightly with wire. Arrange in groups spaced evenly round the circle. Insert the wires between the foliage and take through to the back of the garland. Twist the excess wire over and push back up into the moss to secure. Decorate with a bow of red ribbon. *(Diag. 5.)*

Advent Wreath

Originally a time of fasting, the Advent period has been honoured in the western church since the sixth century. Recently, customs associated with this time have been revived and in Sweden and Germany in particular Advent has become widely celebrated with Advent candles lit in many homes.

No one really knows when the Advent wreath came to Germany but it is thought that it travelled from Sweden, an emulation of the Nordic "Crown of Lights". It became popular soon after the First World War in northern Germany and by the 1930s had spread throughout the entire German-speaking part of Europe.

The wreath is made of interwoven fir twigs and has four candles, one of which is lit for one hour on each Advent Sunday preceding Christmas, until all four burn together.

The Advent wreath seen in the photograph opposite is made in exactly the same way as the evergreen wreath previously described, using small bunches of holly wired onto a background foliage of yew and pine. It has four metal candleholders wired into the moss base and hidden by the foliage.

If using candleholders *(Diag. 6.)* wire them to the wreath after the foliage is in place. Twist over one end *(Diag. 7.)* of a 15 cm (6 in) length of wire and pass it through the hole in the centre of the candleholders. Insert the wire between the leaves and take through to the back of the wreath. Pull tight, making sure that the candleholder sits upright when in position, and twist the excess wire over into the moss to secure. Space the four holders an equal distance apart.

If no holders are available, the candles can be wired directly into the base. Cut a 50 cm (20 in) length of wire and bind round the end of the candle a few times. Turn under at the base and bend over to form a spike approximately 10 cm (4 in) long *(Diag. 8.)*. Pass right through the wreath to the wrong side and twist the excess wire over and push back into the moss.

Always make sure that the candles are standing vertically before lighting and are never left burning unattended.

In German homes the Advent wreath is often suspended from the ceiling by ribbons. Attach four wire loops centrally between the candles on the outer edge of the garland and thread a 135 cm (5 ft) length of ribbon through each one. Gather the eight ends into a knot or bow and suspend from a ceiling hook. Make four separate bows of ribbon and wire into the wreath over the loops where the ribbons are attached.

Kissing Bough

Kissing under the mistletoe seems to have been solely an English custom, despite our reputation for being a cold race. Possibly in origin a sacred gesture of peace, the kissing took place under the Kissing Bough, a huge garland of greenery. As the English predecessor of the Christmas tree, it hung

Diag. 5.   Finish off with groups of berries.

Diag. 6.

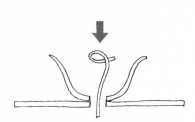

Diag. 7. Wire the candleholders to the wreath after the foliage is in place.

Diag. 8. Secure the candle with strong wire.

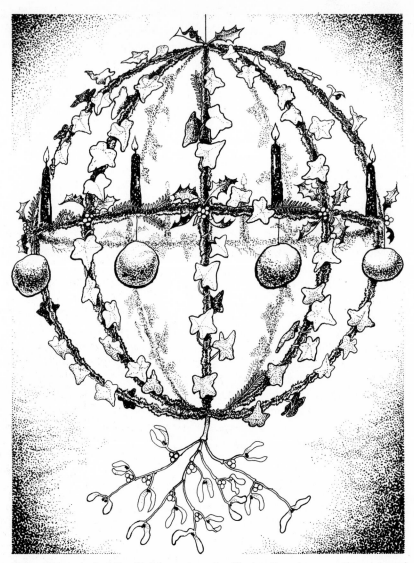

Before the arrival of the Christmas tree, the Kissing Bough was at the centre of Christmas celebrations in England.

from the ceiling of the main living room. The Bough was shaped either like a May garland or a crown and was fashioned from hoops of willow, bound with yew and hung with red apples and candles. From the centre was suspended the traditional bunch of mistletoe. The candles were lit on Christmas Eve and relit each evening until Twelfth Night. The Bough became the focus of all the Christmas celebrations; family and friends sang carols under it, the mummers enacted their plays and the children danced beneath it. Sadly, it was pushed from favour by the Teutonic Christmas tree, although in some remote farms and cottages of north-west England it can still be found in use over the festive season.

As it is to be hung from the ceiling, the bough needs to be as light as possible, so pad the frame with just enough moss to cover and try and find a few crab apples to hang from the bottom as these weigh less than our modern cultivated varieties.

Here are instructions for making a half Bough. If you use an old lampshade frame as a base it can be stripped down and used each year.

You will need:

Cane or wire lampshade frame approx. 40–45 cm (16–18 in) in
    diameter
7 red apples or a mixture of apples and satsumas
7 red candles with candleholders
Sphagnum moss
Small sprigs of evergreen, preferably yew – trim to 8 cm (3 in)
Fine florists wire and red ribbon

To make:

Bind the whole of the frame with moss, using the fine wire to secure. Incorporate any sprigs of evergreen as you work, but keep them short so they never come into contact with the lighted candles. Wire the candleholders to the circular base of the frame, one between each upright.

Suspend the apples and oranges from the bottom of the frame. (Tie a double knot at one end of a 20 cm (8 in) length of coloured string and thread up through the core.)

Hang a bunch of mistletoe from the centre of the frame. Pass a length of ribbon through the struts at the top of the frame and use to suspend the Bough from a ceiling hook.

Cross Stitch Table Garland

Continuing with the winter theme of evergreens and berries, here is an embroidered garland approximately 30 cm (12 in) in diameter, designed as a table centre and worked entirely in a simple cross stitch. It was stitched on a linen fabric which has 8 threads per centimetre and worked in three strands of stranded cotton throughout. Each stitch is worked over two threads each way. The design can be carried out on any embroidery fabric with a larger or smaller number of threads per centimetre and the embroidery cotton altered accordingly.

Cross stitch should always be worked so that the second stitches making the cross are all slanted in one direction, giving the embroidery an even finish. Any stitches which do cross the wrong way will catch the light and show up. Do use an embroidery frame when working as it will keep the fabric taut and easier to work.

To fill in an area of cross stitch, work along the row from right to left and bring the needle up through the fabric at the lower, right hand point of the stitch. Make a row of slanting stitches placed evenly apart, each one over an equal number of threads. Always keep the needle vertical when working. Working from left to right, complete the row of crosses by inserting the needle into the exact holes of the first row. (*Diag. 9.*)

Diag. 9. Work each stitch over an equal number of threads.

You will need:

White linen
Anchor stranded cotton in the following colours: 046 scarlet;
    0335 flame; 0279 light green; 0269 dark green; 0268 moss
    green; 0307 amber gold; 0339 terra cotta; 0218 forest green
Crewel needle and embroidery frame

To make:

Find the centre of the tablecloth by folding it into quarters and
mark with a tacking thread, making a large central cross.
Using the graph as a guide, count the number of threads from
the centre to the bottom point of each heart and mark. This
will act as a guide when stitching. Start by filling in one of the
red hearts with cross stitch and following the patterns on
pages 32 and 33 *(Diag. 10.)* and working from left to right,
complete one half of the garland.

Repeat the design to complete the second half, again
working from left to right. When finished, place on a padded
surface and press on the wrong side with a damp cloth.

Kerstkrans – Dutch Pastry Wreath

Every Dutch child looks forward to December 5th, the eve of
the Feast of St Nicholas or *Sinterklaas* as he is known in
Holland. Sinterklaas bears little resemblance to the jolly Santa
known to the children of England and America, and his
origins can be traced back to the time of the Spanish Moors.
He is a stern yet benevolent bishop, who carries a sack full of
presents to be distributed to all well-behaved children and a
sharp birch rod to punish those who have been naughty.
Always by his side is his servant Black Peter (*Zwarte Piet*) a
Moor, dressed in seventeenth-century Spanish costume.

Preparations for the great event begin ten days beforehand
and each evening the children leave a shoe filled with hay or a

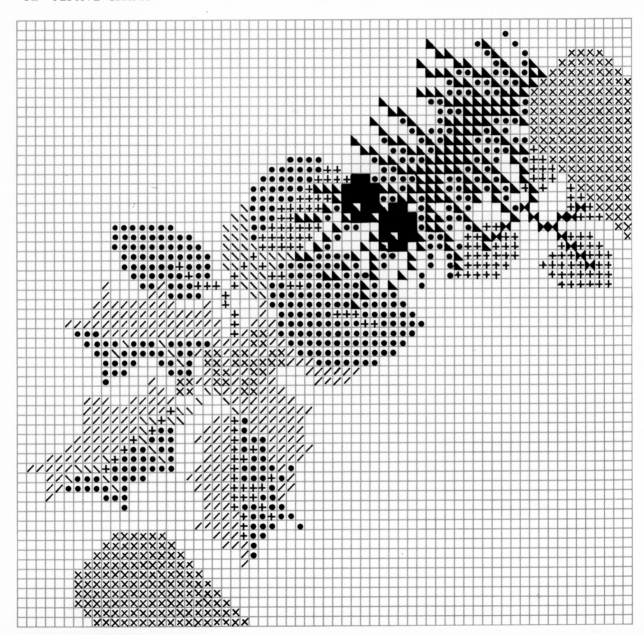

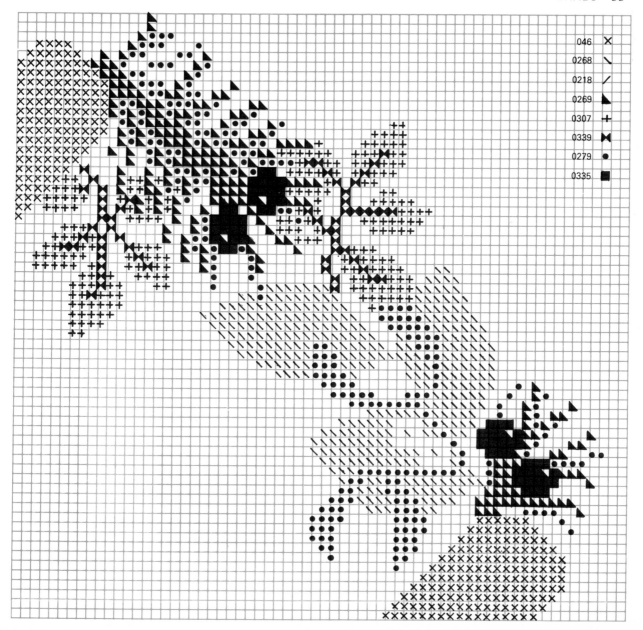

046	✕
0268	╲
0218	╱
0269	◣
0307	✛
0339	▶◀
0279	●
0335	■

carrot, in the hearth to feed Sinterklaas' horse. While Sinterklaas listens down the chimney to check for good behaviour within, Black Peter sees that by morning their offerings are exchanged for a small gift.

To celebrate this festival the Dutch have a renowned pastry which is shaped into the family initials (*Letterbanket*) for Sinterklaas Eve, or into a wreath (*Kerstkrans*) if it is to be eaten as part of the Christmas feast.

Ingredients:
225 g (8 oz) flaky pastry (homemade or deep frozen)
225 g (8 oz) ground almonds
225 g (8 oz) castor sugar
grated rind of ½ lemon
1 drop almond essence
1 beaten egg
2 tbsps sieved apricot jam
1 beaten egg mixed with 1 tbsp cold water for glaze
Flaked almonds – lightly toasted
Red ribbon

Diag. 11.   *Fold the pastry over the almond paste.*

To make:
Thaw out the pastry. Pre-heat the oven to 225°C (425°F), gas 7. Sieve the ground almonds and castor sugar into a bowl. Add the lemon rind. Work in the almond essence and beaten egg to make a smooth almond paste.

Roll the pastry into a strip 14 cm (5½ in) wide and 51 cm (20 in) long, on a lightly floured board. Shape the almond paste into a long roll and place on one side of the pastry. (*Diag. 11.*) Moisten the edges of the pastry with a little water and fold it over the almond paste. Seal the edges well. Make cuts all along the joined edge approximately 2 cm (¾ in) deep and 2 cm (¾ in) apart. Shape the roll into a circle, making sure the join is firmly sealed. Transfer to a floured baking sheet and leave in a cool place for 10 minutes to chill.

Brush with lightly beaten egg and bake for 30 minutes in a

hot oven. The pastry should be golden brown. Transfer the garland carefully onto a cooling rack and glaze immediately with warm apricot jam which has been sieved and thinned with a little water. Decorate with lightly toasted, flaked almonds and just before serving add a bow of red ribbon. (*Diag. 12.*)

Corn Wreath

At the beginning of the Christmas season Danish farmers spread hay on the frozen ground in the forests for the deer to feed on. They also hang out the traditional *Juleneg*, or sheaf of oats, to provide food for the birds. Apart from being a sacrifice to the fertility deity, the Juleneg was thought to be a magic means of protecting the next year's crop from damage by birds. The Norsemen brought the custom to England and in many places garlands of corn are hung on the door at Christmas, an attractive alternative to the usual evergreens. Hang it in a covered porch if you want it to survive twelve days of English weather and if you really want to attract the birds string it with whole peanuts and dried fruit. Unlike most of the traditional cornwork, the wreath is made using dry materials.

Diag. 12. Decorate with lightly toasted almond flakes.

You will need:

Thick galvanized wire, or a 30 cm (12 in) wreath frame
Large bunch of wheat or mixed corn with the stalks trimmed
    to approx. 12 cm (5 in)
Hay for padding the frame
Raffia, large darning needle, fawn button thread, coloured
    ribbon

To make:

Cut the wire into four lengths of 102 cm (40 in). Make each length into a circle 30 cm (12 in) in diameter, twisting the cut

Diag. 13.   Mark top and bottom centres.

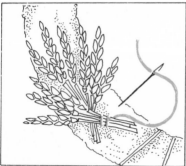

Diag. 14.   Attach the heads of corn in groups of three.

Diag. 15.   Decorate with a group of seed pods or bearded wheat.

ends round each other to secure. Bind the four circles together with Sellotape or raffia. Working on a 10 cm (4 in) section at a time, pad the circle thickly with hay and secure with tightly bound raffia. Mark the top and bottom centres and join with a coloured thread. *(Diag. 13.)* This will act as a guide when stitching the bunches of wheat in place.

Starting at the top left hand side and working downwards, stitch the trimmed wheat to the hay base. Use a darning needle and buttonhole thread and attach the stalks in groups of three, laying them at alternate angles as you would if you were making a plait. *(Diag. 14.)* Work round the base this way until you have reached centre bottom.

Complete the right hand side in the same way, leaving a gap of 7 cm (3 in) at the bottom centre for added decoration. Remove the coloured guide line. Make a small bunch of odd seed pods or heads of corn and stitch to the garland at bottom centre. Thread a loop of raffia at the top, centre back for hanging and finish off with a coloured ribbon. *(Diag. 15.)*

Fir Cone Wreath

Collecting fir cones, nuts and berries to be made into decorations is a favourite game with all children. Collect the cones in the autumn when the winds have brought them down from the trees. If some of the larger ones are not fully opened they can be baked for an hour in a moderate oven. Beechnuts, acorns and sweet chestnuts in their cases make attractive groupings, but make sure they have their stalks intact or they will be difficult to wire. Glue the acorns in their cups or they may drop out.

You will need:

A good selection of assorted cones, pine, larch, anything you can find. Approximately 1¼ kg (2½ lb) in weight

Wire and straw frame 30 cm (12 in) in diameter – as for the
  corn wreath page 35, or a bought frame
Florists stub wires
Clear varnish in an aerosol can

To make:

Construct the base as described for the corn wreath on page
35. Using the florists stub wires, wire the cones singly round
the base, and the small ones in groups of two or three as
previously described for berries and acorns page 26.

To make a flower, cut the inner section out of a large open
cone and spread open the outer scales. (*Diag. 16.*) Glue a tiny
cone or nut in the centre.

Arrange the wired cones in random groups round the base.
Spike the wires into the base and take through to the back.
Twist the excess wire over and push up into the hay base to
secure.

Complete with a coat of clear varnish to bring out the
colours. For a Christmas sparkle smear the tips of the open
cones with glue, then dip in silver or gold glitter. The cones
can be interspersed with small witch balls, groups of beads,
seed heads, anything you choose and of course the wreath
can be stored for use each year as none of the materials will
perish.

Diag. 16. *Make the larger cones into flowers.*

Fabric Wreath

Small cotton prints lend themselves well to the making of a
fabric plait. Combine spots, checks, patchwork prints or try
glitter fabrics if the wreath is to be seen by candlelight at a
winter party.

You will need:

3 strips of cotton dress fabric in three different prints, 140 cm
  × 18 cm (1½ yds × 7 in)

Diag. 17.   Fabric wreath.

90 cm (1 yd) of 5 cm (2 in) width ribbon or equivalent in dress
   fabric for a bow
Off cuts of Terylene wadding for stuffing

To make:

With right sides facing, fold the strips of fabric in half
lengthwise. Giving a 1 cm (⅜ in) seam allowance, stitch down
the length of the strip and across one end. Turn to right side.
Stuff quite lightly with Terylene. Turn in the raw edges of
each strip and close with a slip stitch.

Overlap one end of each of the three padded strips and
stitch together firmly. Plait the three together evenly and
stitch the remaining ends together to secure. Hide the join
with a large, floppy bow. *(Diag. 17.)*

May Garland

At the centre of all the May Day festivities in England is the
Maypole. Originally a whole tree cut down in the forest, it
was trimmed of its branches and carried in procession to the
village green by the young men and girls. Once erected it was
adorned with coloured ribbons and garlands of greenery and
flowers and became the centre round which the early ring
dances were performed. Similar ceremonies take place today,
although it is the very young children who weave the ribbons
as they dance round the pole, unaware of the pagan origins of
rites which began in honour of the sun god, the god of
fertility.

May garlands were fashioned in all shapes and sizes and
the bearers accompanied the daisy-crowned May Queen on
her tour of the parish. A hoop garland was the most common,
made from a light framework of intersecting wooden hoops
bound with leaves and flowers, often with a May Doll, "the
lady", suspended in the middle. In many counties May
Bunches were carried through the streets by the girls. They

ranged from simple posies and willow wands entwined with daisy chains, to cowslip balls hanging from a wooden stave. The girls were usually followed by a band of boys all blowing vigorously on their tin May Horns, ostensibly to welcome summer!

You will need:

2 lengths of thick wire or cane 102 cm (40 in) and 56 cm (22 in) in length
1 broom handle – keep as a stave or cut to suit height of child
1 2.5 cm (1 in) clout nail
Fine florists wire or thick crochet cotton for binding
Emulsion paint, any colour
3.15 m (3½ yds) of 2 cm (¾ in) width coloured ribbon
4 small cat bells
Sphagnum moss
Selection of flowering currant, bluebells, primroses, violets, red campion – a traditional garland flower – and small sprays of greenery

To make:

Pick the blooms in the cool of the day and stand in water for several hours. Ferns and evergreens can be completely immersed in water for an hour or two before use. Bruise or slit the ends of any woody stemmed foliage.

Paint the broom handle. Make two wire circles, one 30 cm (12 in) and one 15 cm (6 in) in diameter, twisting the ends of the wire round each other to secure. Bind each hoop tightly with just enough moss to cover, using the fine wire or crochet cotton to secure. Tie any small flowers together in bunches ready for use.

Bind the background sprays of foliage into the hoops, then attach the flowers in the same way. Tie the larger ones on first, then bunches of small ones spaced evenly round the circle. Keep back a little bunch to make a top knot.

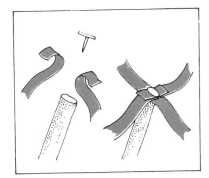

Diag. 18.   Nail the four ribbons to the pole.

Cut the ribbon into four equal lengths. Double over at one end of each piece and attach to the top of the pole with a clout nail. *(Diag. 18.)* Get a helper to support the pole as you work. Hold the small hoop in position approximately 15 cm (5–6 in) from the top of the pole and tie the four ribbons tightly at equal distances apart round the circle. Bring the large hoop up into position, approximately 20 cm (7–8 in) under the small one and tie in place leaving the free ends of the ribbons hanging. Attach a bell to each ribbon end. Tie a small bunch of flowers on the top of the pole. Spray with water to keep fresh. *(Diag. 19.)*

Diag. 19.   Completed May Garland.

In many countries the Easter Hare is thought to bring the eggs.

DECORATING EGGS FOR EASTER

The egg, symbol of life's renewal, was an object of wonder to our primitive ancestors. Long before the Christian Church adopted them as being symbolic of the Resurrection, the egg was held as the embodiment of continuing life by the ancient Greeks, Persians and Chinese. They were borne as gifts at all the great pagan festivals which were held in the spring to celebrate nature's revival after the death of winter.

From Phoenician mythology we learn of the cosmic egg, born of the union of Aer and Aura. From Greek legend we are told of the creation of cosmic matter which finally assumed the shape of an egg, with Night as its shell. Amid the two halves of sky and earth was born Phanes, the Light, and from the union of Phanes and Nux, Night, Heaven and Earth were created.

As far back as 900 BC the Chinese were known to have exchanged red eggs at their spring festival and it is thought that this colour was chosen above all others because, like the egg, it is a symbol of life. In Persia, the spring feast was known as the "Feast of the Red Egg" and red remained the most traditional colour for Easter eggs until well into the Middle Ages. A Polish legend tells of Our Lady painting eggs while at Nazareth to amuse the Infant Jesus, while from Romania comes the belief that the eggs were stained scarlet by the blood of Christ. Pagan or Christian, each civilization has proffered its own story.

By the thirteenth century the custom of exchanging dyed eggs at Easter had spread all over Europe and it was recorded in England in Edward I's household accounts of 1290 that the sum of eighteen pence had been spent on 450 eggs which were to be decorated with gold leaf and distributed to the royal household.

The pagan beginnings of the Easter festival are apparent in the derivation of the word Easter, from Eostre, the Anglo-Saxon goddess of spring, whose celebrations were held about the time of the vernal equinox. Early Christians adopted the festival as their own and called it the Paschal festival, from its association with the Jewish Passover and this link still survives in the north of England where the term Pace-egg, for Easter egg, has slipped into common usage.

Following a Church edict in the fourth century AD, eggs became a forbidden food during the forty austere days of Lent, so it was with great joy that they were restored to the table on Easter Sunday. Taken to the church, they were offered up for blessing by the parish priest and it was during the 1500s that Pope Pius V appointed this prayer for the use of the people of England. "Bless, O Lord, we beseech Thee, this Thy creature of eggs, that it may become a wholesome sustenance to Thy faithful servants, eating in thankfulness to Thee, on account of the Resurrection of Our Lord." After the ceremony the eggs were distributed to relatives, friends and neighbours, the more beautifully decorated ones to be kept and cherished, the others to be used in some of the ritualistic games of the season.

Egg-rolling, still prevalent in the north of the country, is played both on Easter Sunday and Monday and is thought to be symbolic of the stone rolling from the sepulchre at Christ's Resurrection. The coloured, hardboiled eggs are taken to a grassy slope and rolled down it until the shells are broken. They are finally eaten, but much of the fun is drawn from the good luck omens attached to the game, as with the girls of Connel Ferry in Argyll, who believed that the lucky owner of the egg that travelled farthest would be the first to marry! In some parts there are traditional egg-rolling sites used year after year. In Preston in Lancashire it takes place in Avenham

Park, at Penrith in the castle moat and in Edinburgh, on Arthur's Seat.

Whatever Christian significance is attached to the egg-rolling, the bands of northern Pace-eggers of the last century were enacting a far older tradition. These groups of extravagantly dressed mummers, with their blackened faces and cloaks of animal skin, were acting out primitive vegetation rites symbolising the triumph of light over darkness or the rebirth of nature with thanks given to the sun god.

The principal characters of the mumming plays varied little, the main combatants being St George and the Turkish Knight, accompanied by several minor souls who supplied light relief between the action. The stock buffoon was Old Tosspot, whose straw tail filled with pins would tear any hand that grabbed it. They worked to no script, but the rituals enacted were passed orally down the generations and the words known to the last letter.

In some districts the Pace-eggers or Jolly-boys walked the parish, pausing to sing outside each house or farm while Old Tosspot collected Pace-eggs and small gifts in his wicker basket.

Of course, it is inevitable that children will want to know how the Easter eggs arrive and it is the Easter Hare, sacred to the goddess of spring, that is thought to be the bringer of eggs. On Easter morning English children search every corner of house and garden for the secret cache left by the hare. In Yugoslavia they run to the stable to find the sugared eggs in a nest in the hay. In France they are told that the hare ran all the way to Rome to collect them. The Easter bunny or rabbit who performs the task in America is a much later variant on the theme, an example of the confusion which exists in more recent folk beliefs between the hare and the rabbit.

Although the hare continues to be an emblem of Easter it was at one time thought to be associated with witchcraft by those devout Christians who condemned all worship of the early pagan deities. It became the commonest form of familiar taken by witches and in popular tradition replaced the were-wolf which died out after real wolves became extinct in this country.

Attendant superstitions were much in evidence over the spring season and nowhere more so than in the poultry yard. A hundred years ago in rural England the setting of eggs for hatching was riddled with fertility rituals and taboos. It was thought unwise to carry fertile hens' eggs over running water, or to set them on a Sunday, especially in May, the month of witchcraft. Pencilled crosses on the shells saved the eggs from predatory foxes and the last egg laid by an old hen was kept to serve as a fertility charm.

Numbers assumed great importance and only odd amounts were set in the clutch. Flowers too, affected hatching, each yellow bloom representing a chick. Small posies of five or six flowers were unlucky for, by imitation, each hen would hatch that number of eggs. In Somerset farmers' wives never cut daffodils for the house before the geese had hatched their eggs in fear that they may mistake the flowers for goslings and desert the nest.

And so Christian ritual and pagan superstition both continued to enhance and protect the egg, the supreme example of continuing life.

Dyed Eggs

Hardboiled eggs are the easiest to dye and can either be dipped into a prepared dye or, more often, boiled in it. There is less chance of an egg cracking if it is kept at room temperature overnight before use. If possible use only white shelled eggs and the colours will be wonderfully clear and vibrant, although there may be a variation in several eggs immersed in the same dyebath owing to the lime content of the shell which will govern the amount of dye absorbed.

Both edible food dyes and fabric dyes are suitable for bright colours, but the dyes obtained from natural sources such as flowers, leaves, berries, even bark chips, give a softer, gentler colour to the eggs and of course are available to everyone at no cost.

To prepare a natural dye, add the crushed berries or chopped leaves to a saucepan of cold water, bring to the boil and simmer for a while until you get the strength of colour required. Strain and leave to cool.

In England the most commonly used dyes were gorse flowers for a bright yellow, onion skins which produce strengths of yellowy orange to brown, beetroot juice, madder root and cochineal for the reds and spinach leaves which impart green, as do the petals of the Pasque flower, or purple anemone. The fine outer skins of the onion can be wrapped round the eggshell and held in place with cotton to produce a lovely mottled effect.

Add the whole egg, bring to the boil and simmer gently for about thirty minutes to obtain a good colour. Remove from the water, dry thoroughly and while still warm rub the shell with a drop of salad oil on a soft cloth. This will deepen the colour and add lustre to the surface. A few drops of vinegar added to the dye will also brighten the colours.

If you decide to use the more readily obtainable food dyes, just add a few drops to the cold water and boil the eggs as above. When using fabric dyes remember that you will only need a small amount of each colour so there is no need to dissolve and waste a whole tin of dye. Made up, they can be stored in screw top jars and used several times.

The Blocking Technique

This is one of the easiest ways of putting a design on an egg and great fun for small children to try. Collect together some tiny flowers, leaves or grasses, a little salad oil and an old pair of tights. Hardboil an egg and have your dyebath ready.

Dip the flower heads into the oil and arrange on the surface

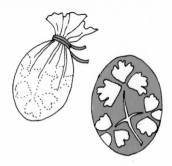

Diag. 1.   The pattern of the leaf will remain.

of the egg. Wrap the egg in a piece of nylon cut from the tights, so that the flowers or whatever else used are pressed firmly against the shell. *(Diag. 1.)* Dye to the desired shade. When the nylon and flowers are removed the imprint will remain.

To Blow an Egg

If you want to keep your decorated eggs indefinitely, it is best to blow out the contents. Keep the egg at room temperature for a while as those taken straight from the refrigerator are difficult to blow.

Using a large, sharp darning needle, carefully pierce an air hole in the pointed end of the egg. Make a slightly larger hole in the flat end, roughly 5 mm (3/16 in) in diameter. Using the needle, break and stir the yolk inside the shell. This will make it easier to get the contents out. Blow into the small hole, forcing the contents out of the larger one. It will probably take more than one breath! Wash the eggshell out immediately, using warm water and detergent and prop it up on a paper tissue to drain and dry. All traces of grease must be removed or the dye won't take to the surface.

To make the fragile shells easier to handle when dipping in the dyes a pipe cleaner or a very fine knitting needle can be inserted through the holes and used as a handle. Finally, when the eggs have been decorated the two holes can be sealed with a blob of wax or a patch of paper coloured to match.

Use the egg carton to store the eggshells until you use them. The yolks can be kept and scrambled for breakfast!

For display purposes the blown and decorated eggs can be suspended on a length of cotton. Tie the cotton to a spent match. Insert the match through the larger hole and turn crossways. Alternatively, tie the cotton to a pretty bead and pull the thread right through the shell. *(Diag. 2.)*

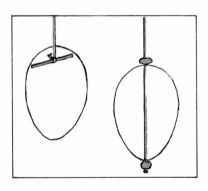

Diag. 2.   The eggs can be suspended.

The Batik Technique

Many of the finest designs using this very old method of decoration come from Eastern and Central Europe, where the decorating of eggs is a traditional peasant art. The intricate designs are drawn onto the eggshell in wax using a special tool called a *stužka*, and the eggs are then dyed in the usual way. This process is repeated several times, working through from the light dyes to the darker ones before finally removing the wax to reveal the multi-patterned egg. The method can be copied very simply using a selection of pins and cut feathers to make the patterns. Simple designs in one colour look the most effective. (Eggs decorated in this way are illustrated on the front of the book.)

You will need:

Several pins with varying sized heads, each one stuck into a
    short length of dowelling for a handle
Goose quills – stripped and cut into shape
Kitchen mug or tin filled with damp sand
An old tablespoon
Candle stub
Mixture of beeswax and paraffin wax in equal amounts
Prepared fabric dyes
Blown eggs
Very fine knitting needle. Small lump of Blu-Tack

To make:

Blow out the contents of the eggs as described on page 48. Prepare the goose feathers. Strip bare the shaft of each quill, leaving about 2.5 cm (1 in) at the tip of the feather. Trim and cut into a shape no more than 1 cm (⅜ in) in length. *(Diag. 3.)* Make several. Bend the handle of the spoon over and embed firmly in the damp sand. Place a small amount of the wax

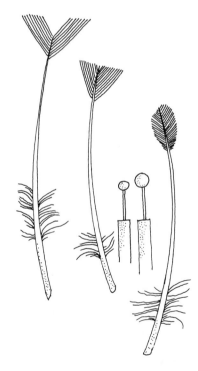

Diag. 3.   Prepared feathers and pins.

Diag. 4.   Heat the wax over a flame.

mixture in the bowl of the spoon and heat over the candle until melted. *(Diag. 4.)*

Pass the fine knitting needle through both holes in the egg, being careful not to damage the shell. A small lump of Blu-Tack wrapped round the needle will prevent the eggshell from moving about should the needle not be a perfect fit.

Use the needle as a handle while decorating the egg. Make a few guidelines on the shell with a pencil if you don't feel confident enough to work your pattern freehand.

To apply the decoration, dip the tip of the feather into the melted wax and touch it quickly to the egg surface to form a shape. (You may find it beneficial to practise on a bit of paper first before beginning work on the egg.) Make the main design by using one or two different feathers or by using just one and altering the direction in which it is laid on the shell. *(Diag. 5.)* Dots and streaks of varying sizes can then be added using the different pinheads. Keep the design as simple as you can, trying not to overlap any of the wax shapes as you apply them or it will look confused and heavy. When finished, clean off any greasy fingerprints from the undecorated areas with methylated spirits. This will ensure an even dyeing.

Warm the dye a little, but to no more than 40°C (104°F) or the wax will melt. Holding the egg by the needle, immerse it in the dye, turning it round until the desired colour is reached. Should the eggs need to be left in the solution for any length of time, as I have found with some of the paler colours, they can be filled with water prior to immersion to give weight and prevent them from floating.

When "cooked" remove with a slotted spoon and pat dry with a tissue. If one colour only is to be used, remove the wax now. Hold the egg against the side of the candle flame and absorb the wax as it melts with a paper tissue. Never try and remove it any other way or you will scratch the design.

As you become more familiar with this method you may want to use several colours. Leave the wax on after the first

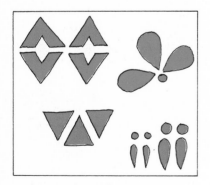

Diag. 5.   Practise making patterns first on paper.

dyeing and add more shapes to the design in the same way. The process can be repeated several times, always working from the palest colours to the dark, i.e. yellows, through oranges and reds to blue and black. After the last dyeing, remove all wax from the egg and buff up the surface with a little salad oil on a soft cloth.

Straw Appliqué

The egg decorators of Czechoslovakia have perfected this technique requiring great patience and skill. The eggs are blown and dyed first and it is important that the ground colour is rich and dark so that it is in sympathy with the natural tones of the straw. The effect comes both from the pattern of the cut shapes and the direction in which they are laid, so that the light catches the grain. Straw has a natural shine which never deteriorates with age.

You will need:

A blown egg
Sharp scissors
Clear adhesive
Natural straw – either freshly gathered or available in packs at most handicraft shops. Wheat, oats and rye are all suitable.

To make:

Prepare the straw. All the nodes should be cut out and the remaining pieces soaked in warm water for about an hour. Slit each straw down one side with a sharp blade and flatten on the inside with a blunt knife. Put some pressure on the knife and draw the whole length of the straw towards you. Do not iron it or it will become too brittle and dry and will not curve to the shape of the egg.

As the nature of the materials virtually dictates that the designs are regular in format, it is best to work to a few

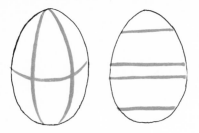

Diag. 6.   Divide into sections.

Diag. 7.

Diag. 8.   Work from the centre outwards.

guide-lines marked lightly in pencil before you begin. Work your design out on paper first, then divide the egg into sections accordingly. Perhaps two vertical bands crossed at top and bottom to give four segments, or a horizontal division running round the centre of the egg dividing it in two *(Diag. 6.)*. Lines radiating out from a central star may also be helpful. *(Diags. 7 & 8.)*

Using sharp scissors, cut the straw into small shapes – triangles, diamonds of different sizes, narrow strips and tiny circles. Cover the back of each shape lightly with glue, position on the egg and slide it gently into place with the aid of a pin. Press down using a soft cloth.

Painted Eggs and Ethnic Design

At the beginning of this century professional egg decorators were to be found in most villages in Poland, Hungary and Czechoslovakia. Many of the designs they used were stylized and mixed the Christian symbols of the church with the earlier pagan emblems of healing and new life. Whether handpainted or waxed and dyed, the basic symbols put onto the eggs contained the same message: the sun for good fortune, flowers for love and charity and an endless line for eternity.

Birds featured prominently in the designs, the Phoenix being the most widely used. According to legend it lived for five hundred years in the Arabian wilderness, then was consumed to ashes on a funeral pyre made from gums and spices and lit by the beating of its own wings. It rose from the ashes to live again and in Medieval Christian writings was depicted as a symbol of the Resurrection.

The letters XV, meaning *Christos Vaskrese*, usually appear on Yugoslavian eggs. This means "Christ is Risen", the traditional Easter Day greeting in the Eastern European countries. Young and old exchange kisses and the reply, "He is risen indeed" is given. On the wooden eggs from Russia it is XB

A collection of hand-painted eggs.

Diag. 9.   A bird design from Germany painted on a goose egg.

and on those from Poland appear the sign of the Cross or the Fish.

Perhaps the easiest way for the beginner to apply surface decoration is to paint it on, rather than get involved with a more intricate technique such as batik. Poster paint holds endless possibilities for experimentation with pattern and can be applied with different shaped brushes, pointed or flat ended. The more subtle colours found in the water colour palette lend themselves to finer work and can be used to copy some of the delicate flower and bird designs so loved by the egg decorators of Hungary. *(Diag. 9.)*

Whichever you decide to use, the paint can only be applied successfully to a grease-free surface so clean the eggshell with methylated spirits first. Map out your designs lightly with a fine pencil, then use a series of fine water colour brushes to complete the painting. Spray with a matt varnish to seal and preserve.

Blackbirds Eggs in a Nest

Fifty or sixty years ago, before we were overwhelmed by the chocolate egg, clutches of little sugared eggs could be bought in the shops at Easter time. Usually made of marzipan, they were coloured pink and blue and stippled to resemble wild birds eggs. They were usually displayed in a nest. A charming gift, they are easily made by children as no cooking is involved. Because they are made from uncooked fondant, they should be eaten within three days. The nest can be edged with a few candied primroses, as in the photograph on page 27.

The Nest

You will need:

Small amount of clean hay

Matching button thread and a darning needle
A few duck feathers and a little moss

To make:

Sort out the hay and gather about a dozen of the longest
strands into a bunch. Flatten one end into a coil like the centre
of a small raffia mat. Using the darning needle and button
thread, secure with a double stitch. This will form the flat base
of the nest.

Working from right to left, continue to coil the hay round
the base bringing the sides up gradually as you work. Secure
with a blanket stitch every 2 cm (¾ in), taking the needle
through each stitch in the *previous row* to hold in place. Join in
more hay where necessary by overlapping the ends slightly.
Finish off with a double stitch on top. Line the nest with goose
feathers or some dry moss and decorate the edge with fresh or
edible candied primroses.

Fondant Eggs

Quantities given are for approximately 35 eggs.

Ingredients:

225 g (8 oz) sifted icing sugar, plus some extra for kneading
1 tbsp egg white
1 tbsp golden syrup
Peppermint flavouring (optional). Blue and brown food
colouring

To make:

Separate the egg white from the yolk and set aside one
tablespoon of the white. Keep the remainder for the candied
flowers. Sift the icing sugar into a large bowl. Add the golden
syrup and sufficient egg white to give a pliable mixture. Add a

few drops of peppermint essence. Knead well on a board dredged with icing sugar until the fondant becomes smooth and easy to handle. Add a few drops of blue food colouring and knead into the mixture until you have an even colour. Cut the fondant into about 35 even pieces and shape into eggs. (Keep your hands dusted with icing sugar.)

To add speckles to the eggs, spray lightly with brown food colouring flicked off an old toothbrush which has been thoroughly washed. Leave to harden for about five hours, then arrange in the nest.

Candied Primroses

Gather a few primroses, the remaining egg white, castor sugar and a small paint brush.

To make:

Choose fresh flowers that are wide open. Make sure the petals are not bruised. Cut the stalks short.

Hold the flower by the stalk and paint with beaten egg white, first the backs of the petals, then the front. Sprinkle all over with castor sugar and place face upwards on a cake rack to dry. Put them in the airing cupboard overnight and they will become quite hard and dry.

The Chocolate Egg

The chocolate egg, a substitute for the traditional dyed egg, is a comparatively recent innovation, probably only 150 years old. The idea of grinding cocoa beans to make a drink originated in Mexico, then passed to Spain during the sixteenth century. A hundred years later it had spread across Europe where chocolate became a socially acceptable drink. Chocolate houses where people could meet and talk had sprung up in several towns in England but it wasn't until the mid-eighteenth century that chocolate became available in solid form.

European confectioners, already artists in the use of fondant and marzipan, began to produce chocolate Easter eggs, each one individually moulded and decorated with elaborate flowers of sugar icing. Their popularity soared as they became machine made and cheaper versions were turned out in their thousands to be available to all.

You will need:

Metal or plastic mould, in two halves
125 g (4 oz) confectioners chocolate – this will make four life-size eggs
Pastry brush. Double saucepan (or small basin and one saucepan)
Edible decorations of choice (crystallised flowers, royal icing, etc.)
Coloured ribbon and cellophane

To make:

Break the chocolate into small pieces and melt in the top of a double saucepan or in a basin over hot water (*not* boiling). Stir until free of lumps but do not overheat. Using the pastry brush, coat the inside of the mould thickly with chocolate and chill until set. Repeat three or four times until the chocolate begins to come away from the edge of the mould. Press the mould at one end and the chocolate shell will drop out. Handle very carefully as any finger marks on the surface cannot be removed. Join the two halves with melted chocolate using your pastry brush, chill until set then decorate as desired. A band of piped icing or chocolate shapes can be used to hide the join and sugared flowers can be stuck on with a dab of melted chocolate. Wrap the finished egg in cellophane and tie with a ribbon.

The egg can also be filled with homemade sweets wrapped in coloured foil.

Chocolate Egg with Nuts

Chocolate eggs of a different kind can be made using real eggshells as a mould. Enough shells can be collected quite quickly if you can persuade the whole family to have omelette for breakfast for a couple of days. A fun project for children who want to make their own Easter gifts.

You will need:

Eggshells
Plain or milk chocolate
Finely chopped hazelnuts or almonds, approx. 1 tsp to each
     25 g (1 oz) of chocolate (optional)

To make:

Pierce an air hole in the flat end of the egg with a darning needle. Using a sharp handicraft blade, carefully enlarge the hole to 1 cm (⅜ in) in diameter. Break the yolk with the needle, pour out the contents and set aside for cooking. Rinse out the shell immediately in warm water and detergent, then leave to drain. When thoroughly dry, stand the eggshells in an egg carton, with the holes uppermost.

Melt the chocolate as previously described and stir in the finely chopped nuts. Using a small funnel, pour the melted chocolate into the eggshell. *(Diag. 10.)* If using nuts, it may be necessary to use a teaspoon as the mixture may not pour easily. After about 30 minutes when the mixture has sunk a little top up again until completely full. Leave to harden for a couple of hours, then carefully peel off the shell.

Wrap the eggs in coloured foil, or decorate with nuts and sugared flowers stuck on with a dab of melted chocolate and present in a nest of straw.

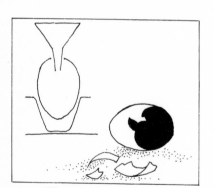

Diag. 10.   Pour the melted chocolate into the eggshell.

Chicken Egg Cup

Again this is really for children to make and can be teamed up with a chocolate egg and given as an Easter gift.

You will need:

Wooden egg cup with a shaped foot
Packet of self-hardening clay
Old kitchen knife or small modelling tool
Poster or acrylic paint
Clear varnish

To make:

When using self-hardening clay it is important to follow the manufacturer's instructions as some are worked completely dry and others with wet fingers.

To form the body of the chicken, take a lump of clay and flatten to a thickness of 5 mm (³⁄₁₆ in). Wrap round the bowl of the egg cup. Smooth over at the rim and foot. Shape two pieces of clay approximately 1.5 cm (½ in) thick into a head and tail and attach to the body. Wings can also be added separately or painted on later. Smooth over the joins using a modelling tool and pinch out the clay to shape the beak, comb and tail feathers. Leave to harden for a couple of days and fill in any cracks that have appeared with a little extra clay.

When completely hardened, paint the chicken and foot of the egg cup, leave to dry before adding the features with a fine brush. Complete with a coat of matt varnish to seal and preserve. (*Diag. 11.*)

Diag. 11.   Colour the chicken with poster paint.

The Easter Tree and Easter Bird

Witches play a large role in the Swedish Easter tradition and in almost every home can be found an Easter tree made from birch twigs and hung with small figures of witches, coloured eggs and feathered birds. Birch is used because it is symbolic of an old Good Friday ritual when members of a family would beat each other with birch switches in memory of Christ's suffering.

During the period when it was believed that witches really existed, they were thought to attend church on Easter Sunday. Eggs were employed to detect their presence and three in the pocket enabled the carrier to see the witches and hear them reciting their prayers backwards. Today, children go round in disguise on Easter Eve, little girls with sooty faces and broomsticks, a reminder of the Easter hag once thought to fly to Brocken on Maundy Thursday to confer with the Devil.

The Swedes arrange their birch twigs in a vase of water to represent a tree. In Germany a much more formal arrangement is constructed from wooden rods covered in greenery and hung with eggs and little dough animals. The Easter birds can be suspended from the tree or hung separately as a mobile.

You will need:

Large chicken or duck egg – blown as described on page 48
Assorted feathers – ask the poulterer to save you a few small, body feathers from a white chicken or some patterned ones from a cock pheasant
Poster or acrylic paint
Scraps of stiff paper in chosen colour
Glue, tracing paper and scissors

To make:

Paint the eggshell all over and leave to dry. Trace the pattern shapes from *Diag. 12.* and transfer onto stiff paper folded double. Cut out. Draw and paint the features on both sides of the bird's head. Join at the beak with a dab of glue.

Arrange three or four feathers on one side of each wing shape and glue in place. Glue feathers in place on one side of

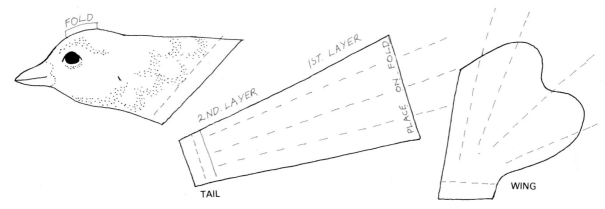

Diag. 12. Glue the feathers along the guidelines.

the tail shape in two layers. Glue a few smaller feathers on the underside of the tail. *(Diag. 12.)*

Fold over the tabs at the neck of the bird, glue in position on the flat end of the egg. Use the blowing hole as a centre guide point. Paint over the glued join to match the body. Attach the tail in the same way, using the other pin hole as a guide. The tail should be placed horizontally to the egg so that the long tail feathers are on top. Paint over the tabs. To attach the wings, turn the tabs up out of sight and glue both the tab and the paper underside of the wing to the egg. This will keep the wings upright.

Finally, make a knot in one end of a length of cotton and glue centrally to the bird's back to suspend.

Palmpasen – Dutch Palm Cross

On the Sunday before Easter, groups of Dutch children parade to the local hospital or old people's home to distribute gifts and to show the old and sick that they have not been forgotten at Easter time. The custom is most popular in the Catholic towns and villages and each one of the children carries their own handmade palm cross in the parade. The crosses are decorated with spring flowers and strung with garlands of dried fruit. On top is an Easter cockerel or Easter hare made from dough.

Keep back some of the dough used for making the hot cross buns or Easter bread and let the children make the cockerel while the baking is being done. Bear in mind when cutting out the shapes that the dough will be double the size after baking.

You will need:

2 pieces of bamboo or wooden dowelling, 45 cm (11 in) and 30 cm (12 in)
Spring flowers and leaves
Raisins, dried fruit
Chicken feathers, button thread
Dough as for hot cross buns or bread – approx. 125 g (4 oz)

To make the cockerel:

Using *Diag. 13.* as a guide, make the dough into a cockerel. Roll out to a thickness of 1 cm (⅜ in) and approx. 13 cm (5 in) square. Using a sharp knife, cut the head and body shape first, then make a fan for the tail. Make three or four long cuts in the fan shape and roll the end of each one round into a curl to make the tail feathers. Add a curl of dough for the wing and some texture on his breast. (I used the point of a small kitchen funnel.) Use a currant for the eye. Leave to rise in a warm place for 30 minutes until double in size, then bake until golden brown.

Glaze with hot golden syrup as soon as it comes from the oven. When cool spear onto the top of the cross.

To make the cross:

Join the two pieces of bamboo together to form a cross and secure with button thread. Decorate with leaves and spring

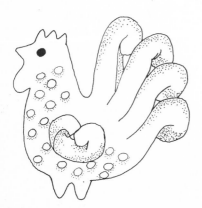

Diag. 13.   Cut out using a sharp knife.

flowers bound on with thread. Add a few chicken feathers if you have some. Thread the raisins and dried fruit together and suspend from the arms of the cross. Secure at the centre point. Lastly, spear the bread cockerel onto the top of the cross. *(Diag. 14.)*

Easter Bread

For many years the Christian Church observed a strict fast during the forty days of Lent, so it was natural that the arrival of Easter should be welcomed with much joy and feasting. Each country has its own special fare, with the Paschal lamb taking pride of place on the table. Eggs feature in all the great national dishes. In Greece and Italy they are served with the main course of lamb, in Hungary in an egg soup, in Portugal as a sweet in the form of fine strands of egg yolk called Angel's Hair.

Second only to the Paschal lamb is the Easter bread, which in many countries served to display the traditional red egg. Known as "Red Thursday", Maundy Thursday is the day for dyeing the eggs and baking the loaves. English families delight in the hot cross buns served fresh from the oven on Good Friday morning, and although they have taken on great Christian significance, their origins stretch back to pre-Christian times when small wheaten cakes were eaten at the spring festivals. Both Greeks and Romans offered these tiny cakes marked with a cross to be eaten at the festivals celebrated at the time of the vernal equinox.

Many of the Easter breads and cakes are made into special shapes, such as chickens, nests, hares and little men *(Diags. 15 & 16.)*, most of which incorporate the red egg as part of the design. The ingredients used vary widely, as do the shapes, but here is a basic milk bread recipe suitable for all the designs.

Prepare the red eggs first. Hardboil them in water to which a little red food colouring has been added.

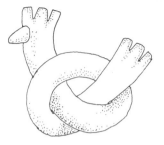

Diag. 14. *An easy way to make a chicken as an alternative way to decorate the Palmpasen.*

Diag. 15.

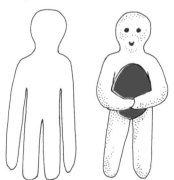

Diag. 16.

Diag. 17. Decorate with poppy seeds.

Ingredients:

540 g (1 lb) strong white flour
1 level tsp salt
1 level tsp sugar
275 ml (½ pt) milk – warmed to 40°C (104°F)
15 g (½ oz) fresh yeast
Beaten egg for the glaze
Poppy seeds for topping (optional)

To make:

Sift the flour and salt into a bowl. To activate the yeast, dissolve the sugar in the milk and use two or three tablespoons to mix the yeast into a smooth paste. Add the remaining milk. Make a well in the flour and pour in the liquid. Mix into a dough, using a wooden spoon. Knead on a floured board until elastic. Cover with greased polythene and put into a warm place to prove until it has doubled in size. Put the dough back onto the board and knock down to release any air bubbles.

Divide into three equal portions. Roll each one into a long sausage. Moisten one end of each strand and press together to join. Plait the three together loosely, incorporating the egg into the centre strand of the plait. Seal and press the ends together. Place on a greased baking tray, brush with beaten egg and sprinkle with poppy seeds. *(Diag. 17.)* Leave to rise for a further 30 minutes before baking for 30–35 minutes at 220°C (425°F), gas mark 7.

The Last Load was brought home in triumph.

HARVEST HOME

Since pagan times man's life has followed the natural rhythms of the rural calendar. The first one, the pastoral calendar was divided according to the old Celtic quarter days round which the animals were husbanded. Later, the agricultural calendar marked with its own quarter days the sowing and harvesting of crops. The pastoral and agricultural cycles eventually merged, although the old feast days remained and were celebrated under new names. In due course Christianity added its blessing, but the seasonal rituals lingered on and stayed part of everyday rural life. In the second half of the year various crops, not just the all-important corn, were harvested with ceremony. The accompanying rites and rituals stemmed both from the magic and superstition of early mythology and from a sound observation of plants and an affinity with nature.

The Chinese recognized a god of the soil whom they invoked at convenient times of the year. They also worshipped a god of ploughing and during the appropriate festival, the emperor himself was known to have stood behind the plough to draw the first furrow.

The Slav farmers believed that every field was ruled by a *Polevik*, a mischievous divinity whose appearance varied according to region. Sometimes he was clothed in white, at others he had a body black as the earth with two eyes of different colours. In place of hair this little deformed dwarf sported a mass of long green grass.

Each agricultural race had its Earth Mother, who guarded the fate of indigenous crops. Just as Ceres looked after the wheat and barley of Europe, so did Chicome Couatl personify the maize of the Americas and the *padi-pĕngantèn*, the Rice Bride, represent the rice spirit of Java.

Remnants of the ancient superstitions which ensured the land's fertility are still to be found on many English farms. The soil, the weather, the time and method of sowing all had their place in folklore and some of the names have survived to remind us. Sterile fields were given suitable titles: Bare Bones, Empty Purse, Labour-in-Vain, just as good land earned praise: Fillpockets, New Delight, Pound of Butter or Land of Promise. The ploughman knew the soil and how to work it. The old reverence for iron and the Christian respect for Fridays were not to be mixed so on that day of the week no ploughing or reaping were ever begun. Saints' days were thought favourable for sowing as were the first days of a new moon for as the moon grew full, so would the seeds swell and prosper by imitation: The moon was thought to have control over many things as diverse as mushroom gathering and the mating of horses!

In certain counties of England the previous year's Corn Dolly was taken from the farm kitchen on Plough Monday and turned in the first furrow where it lay ready to work the magic necessary for the following harvest. Once sown, the seed was encouraged by ceremonies rich and various and again the principle of imitative magic was applied to ensure a fruitful year. In parts of Europe dancing or leaping high in the air was thought to make the crops grow tall. Our own Morris dancers play a similar role, their white clothes attracting the sun to the land, the clashing of their sticks to shake the soil and the high leaps in anticipation of the height of the corn.

Come August, the first crops were maturing. Lavender was cut in the country villages and taken to London to be sold. The candle rushes from the Broads were peeled and dried and packed into bundles ready for Norwich Rush Fair which was held on the first Monday of the month. In the hop fields of Worcestershire the symbolic death and rebirth of the harvest was enacted by a man and a woman buried in hops in a great wicker basket. But, most important of all and essential to man's survival, the corn was harvested.

Before the advent of mechanization which speeded up the process, every man, woman and child became available to help at the corn harvest, the highlight of the farming year. It often spanned four to six weeks during which the helpers prayed for good weather, for each day's delay brought expensive losses.

Towards the end of the nineteenth century the self-binders came into common use, but previous to that the corn was cut by scythe and sickle. The harvest "Lord", his badge of office a trail of green bindweed and red poppies round his wide brimmed hat, led the team of reapers. He set the pace, negotiated payments and later presided at the harvest supper.

The age-old rites of harvest remained along with hand reaping, the most significant concerning the last sheaf. Customs varied from county to county, but whether reaping in lines or in a steadily decreasing circle, the last few ears were left uncut and were thought to embody the spirit of the corn. The stalks were tied or plaited together and as the reapers stood round in a wide semi-circle, they each threw their sickles at the corn so that the responsibility of the final cut lay with no one man.

With the mowing finished, the custom of Crying the Neck was observed on most farms. The last ears to be cut were gathered into a bundle and held up high by the Harvest Lord with a triumphant shout to all that the last corn had been cut and the first part of the harvest successfully completed. These stalks were eventually fashioned into the Corn Dolly or Kern Baby, as she was known and proudly carried home on top of the last load in a great haywain decorated with flowers and pulled by four garlanded horses. Little boys rode on top among the sheaves, a young girl in a white dress and straw bonnet astride the leading horse, while the men walked beside, pitchforks over shoulders, tired but full of joy for the huge task completed. Many of the larger farms were decorated at the entrance with arches of evergreens and flowers, the whole display topped with a crossed sickle and scythe hung with golden corn.

Day-long preparations had produced a magnificent Harvest Supper and so the evening was spent in feasting and singing and celebration, for after Christmas it was the most important meal of the rural year. Roast beef and boiled hams were brought to the table, unlimited supplies of beer and cider, plum puddings and apple pies, all supplementing the usually meagre diet of the farm labourer.

The Harvest Festival we know today, which is associated with the church, is quite a recent occurrence. In 1843 the vicar of Morwenstow in Cornwall revived the old Lammas thanksgiving and it has now become an accepted part of both the church and the agricultural year. The ancient Lammas "Festival of First Fruits" as it was known, was held on August 1st and was a purely sacred occasion. As one of the four agricultural festivals of the year, it takes its name from the Anglo-Saxon *hláfmaesse* or "loaf-mass" at which loaves of bread made from the first ripened corn were consecrated. Later, after it was Christianised, it inevitably became associated with the more recent Harvest Festival which is celebrated today.

The weaving of corn dollies is a specialised art, but here are three examples which are relatively easy to make and will serve as an introduction to straw work.

SUITABLE TYPES OF STRAW

The most suitable straw for making corn dollies is long and flexible, with a thin-walled, hollow stem. All the old varieties had these characteristics, but they are fast disappearing in favour of the short stalked corn grown by the farmers of today. Both soil and climate affect the properties of the growing corn, resulting in straw of widely differing quality across the country.

The varieties which are easily worked and plait well are

Maris Widgeon, Maris Ranger, Dove, Eclipse, Elite Lepeuple, Flamingo and Square Head Master. These are all wheat but oats, rye, barley and the decorative black-bearded wheat imported from Africa can be used. Wild oats too can be incorporated in the corn dollies, although they are regarded as intrusive weeds in the wheat field.

The time for cutting the corn is about a fortnight prior to harvest, when the ears are still upright and it is just turning from green to gold. If cut on the turn, the grain will not fall out when the straw is being worked. Most farmers, if approached directly, will be pleased to give or sell a sheaf for plaiting, but do insist on doing the cutting yourself so you can choose undamaged stems. Cut the corn about 15–20 cms (6–8 in) from the ground, using a sickle or clippers and spread it out to dry in the sun for two or three days on a tarpaulin. It can then be hung in bunches with the ears hanging downwards and stored well away from attack by mice and birds until needed.

If gathered for immediate use, corn cut from the field needs little preparation other than cutting at the first joint and stripping off the leaf sheath. That which has been in store will need soaking in cold water for about an hour. Straw from the previous year will require a few more hours in water to make it flexible. Test for pliability by bending the straw into a "V" and if it springs apart without cracking when released, then it is ready for use. Always keep the tempered straw wrapped in a damp cloth or towel while working, as it will quickly dry out at room temperature.

The Harvest Maid

Whether kept as a rough sheaf or fashioned into the shape of the Earth Mother herself, the spirit of the corn was thought by primitive people to reside in the last stalks cut at the harvest. It is this image of the corn goddess that lies in the origin of the corn dollies we see today.

The Harvest Maid. A Harvest Maid from Launceston in Cornwall with her head of oats and barley.

She was known by several names, Demeter, Isis, Ceres, all names for the one corn spirit round which the harvest rituals were woven. In Greek mythology Demeter was regarded as the Mother, last year's old corn, and Persephone her daughter as the new corn of the year. The myth tells of Persephone's annual death and her mother's mourning, a parallel with the yearly cycle of seedtime and harvest.

In most countries where cereals were grown, fertility rites which centred round the last sheaf were enacted at harvest time. It is thought that the very first corn dollies were made in ancient Egypt where the wheat and barley grew wild. The early nomadic farmers travelled west, taking with them their pagan beliefs and it is from these origins that our own harvest ceremonies are derived.

In Britain the sheaf was made into the figure known variously as the Harvest Maid, Kern Baby or Bride of the Corn, which was kept all year until replaced by the corn dolly from the next harvest. During the eighteenth and nineteenth centuries in England an abundance of designs for corn dollies evolved, each one characteristic of its county of birth and reflecting an aspect of country life. Old style makers of dollies observed a strict code of colours when trimming their work. The traditional ribbons used were white for the virgin corn, green to represent the Spring and the growing seed, red and blue for the familiar poppies and cornflowers which grew alongside the corn. A golden ribbon represents the ripe corn and a brown one the earth that brought forth the seed.

Here is a pattern for a Harvest Maid, the original of which was made in Cornwall. (See drawing on page 72.) It was made from Maris Widgeon wheat, which has a long stem and large head.

You will need:

Brown paper. Strong glue. Lightweight cardboard – shirt box cardboard is ideal. Protractor and ruler.

Approx. 60 mixed straws with heads – wheat, oats, black
   bearded wheat or grasses. Keep dry
12 damp straws without heads for the arms
12 damp straws with heads for the plaits
A few spare straws for skirt decoration
30 cm (12 in) galvanized wire
1 m (1 yd) of 2.5 cm (1 in) width golden ribbon
Raffia or matching button thread for tying

To make the cone:

The Harvest Maid will be more durable if she is made round a
cardboard cone so that she can stand. The old cardboard
spools from cotton factories are ideal for this use. However,
for those who have to make their own here are the instructions for making a cone 18 cm (7 in) high. The pattern is
adjustable and will give a base up to 9 cm (3½ in) in diameter.
Make it from brown paper first and adjust the height and
width to suit the length of straws used for the Maid's body.

Cut a rectangle of brown paper, 35 cm × 30 cm (14 in ×
12 in). Fold in half widthways. Draw out the pattern from
Diag. 1. Cut out. Open out and transfer to card. Cut all round,
then fold into a cone, securing at the top and bottom with
paper clips. Adjust the base width when the body of the Maid
has been completed in straw. Glue the card between the two
paper clips. Leave to dry completely before use, then remove
the clips.

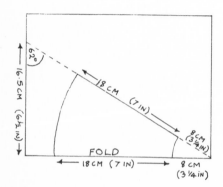

*Diag. 1.   The cone can be made taller
by adjusting the length of the sides.*

To make the Harvest Maid:

Have ready approx. 60 mixed straws with heads. All these
will be used dry and cut at the first joint.

Arms are made with a further 12 damp straws, 30 cm (12 in)
long. Pass a fine wire through the length of one of them. Then
tie all the straws together in the middle and at elbows and
wrists. Leave under a damp cloth.

For the rope plaits that go over her shoulders you will need
12 damp straws with heads, six for each plait. Tie six straws

tightly together at varying heights. Stagger them slightly, making the end of the longest stem 5 cm (2 in) from the tie. Repeat with the other six straws to match. Hold with the left thumb and first finger and divide. Twist the upper straws away from you *(Diag. 2.)* (count four to help keep the twists regular). Bring the twisted straws down over the lower straws. *(Diag. 3.)* Move the left thumb forward and repeat the twist with what are now the new upper straws. Make sure the plait keeps the same width throughout. There is no need to join in extra straws as both plaits need only be 6.5 cm (2½ in) long. When finished, tie off, but do not cut off the ends of the stalks. Keep them damp while assembling the Maid.

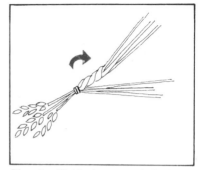

Diag. 2.   Divide the straws in half.

Tie the 60 dry straws together just under the heads and again 2 cm (½ in) down for her neck. Open up her body from the side and insert the arms. Tie again tightly under the arms. Cover the cone with adhesive and quickly push it up the centre of the straws as far as the last tie. Arrange the straws equally round the cone (an elastic band helps to keep them in place). If there are any gaps push up a headless, dry straw. Trim the straws to the edge of the cone. Leave until the straws have adhered and then start to make the decorative plait that goes round the skirt. Make a simple straw hair plait. Work damp and make it 27 cm (10½ in) long. Pull the arms of the Maid into shape. Arrange the two rope plaits over her shoulders, the heads to the front and hanging down her skirt. Tie to the body at the neck.

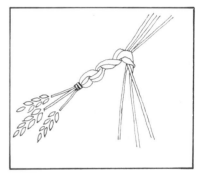

Diag. 3.   Making the rope plait.

Glue the decorative plait in position 1.2 cm (½ in) from the bottom of the skirt. Arrange a small sheaf of mixed, dried flowers and corn together and attach to one side of the Maiden's arms. Finally, tie a bow of golden ribbon at her neck.

Barley Wreath

In parts of France the Corn Maiden is replaced by a wreath made from the first cut corn of the harvest. In Lorraine it is decorated with flowers and ribbons and offered to the mis-

Diag. 4.   *Conceal the wire among the stalks.*

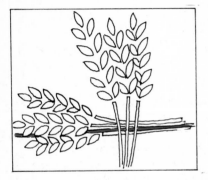

Diag. 5.   *Place the first group at right angles.*

tress of the house. In Pas-de-Calais the wreath is strung with cornflowers and poppies, the red flower held by the corn goddess Ceres and once thought by the Romans to represent the spilt blood of their gods. After being blessed by the priest, the wreath is hung from the ceiling of the farmhouse and the old one taken down, pulled apart and thrown into the barn to ensure fertility for the coming year.

The heart-shaped wreath on page 58 was made from barley but for a complete beginner wheat is easier to work with as the stems are not so fragile. The completed heart is 25 cm (10 in) in diameter.

You will need:

Approx. 200 heads of six-row or ordinary barley – do not trim the stalks but leave as long as possible
Thick galvanized wire in two lengths of 60 cm (24 in)
Clothes pegs. Small amount of raffia. Coloured ribbon

To make:

Prepare the barley or wheat as described on page 71. If using barley keep the stalks as long as possible and strip off the leaf. If using wheat, use only the top part of the stem cut just above the first leaf node. Keep in a damp cloth to retain moisture while working.

Take four heads of barley in your left hand and hold horizontally with heads to the left and with the length of wire concealed among the stalks. *(Diag. 4.)* This will form the base on which you work. Now add the barley in groups of three, working from left to right.

Place a group of three on top, with stalks crossing at right angles and heads vertical to the base. *(Diag. 5.)*

Bend the stalks back under the wire, up to the left of the heads and over to the front of the base so that all the stalks are running parallel. *(Diag. 6.)* Hold firmly at the join with your left hand as you work.

As you continue to add the barley in groups of three all the stalks will be incorporated into the base. Space them evenly along the wire about 1.5 cm (¾ in) apart, until you have covered about 55 cm (22 in). *(Diag. 7.)* If you need to pause while working, use a clothes peg to hold the barley firmly in place. To finish off, bind the stalks to the base with raffia just under the last group of barley and trim. There should be a little wire left free and uncovered at each end for joining.

Cover the second length of wire in the same manner, but reverse the order of working from right to left so that the fatter part of the armature is at the base of the heart.

To complete, shape each section very gently into a half heart shape. Twist the wires over at the back to join the two sections together and bind over the joins with raffia. Leave on a flat surface to dry.

Tie on a loop of raffia at the back for hanging. Assemble two small groups of barley heads and attach over the joins at top and bottom. Decorate with a blue ribbon and cornflowers and poppies if you have them.

Scandinavian Yule Goat

In northern and central Europe the last sheaf was destined to become the Yule straw and was put away until Christmas. In most countries grain from the sheaf was incorporated in the Christmas loaf. In Denmark the loaf was baked in the shape of a boar, which was yet another embodiment of the corn spirit. In Sweden it is fashioned into the *julbock*, a goat made from the dressed stalks and bound with red ribbon, which is stationed under the tree or on the Christmas table for the duration of the festival.

They can be made any size by varying the length and number of straws in the bundle. For a large, standing goat use the full length of the stalk, for a tree decoration use only the top joint.

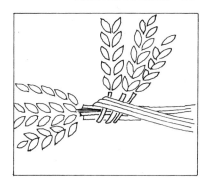

Diag. 6.   Bring the stalks over to the front.

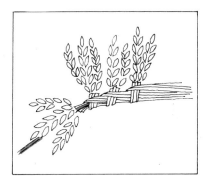

Diag. 7.   Space the groups evenly.

You will need:

A bundle of straws – remove heads and soak as previously
    described
A few heads of rye or wheat for the goat's beard
Fawn button thread
Red ribbon, 1 cm (⅜ in) in width

To make:

Gather together a good bundle of dampened straws roughly
the same length from which the heads have been cut. Using a
double thickness of button thread, tie firmly in two places,
dividing the bundle into three equal parts. *(Diag. 8.)*

Divide the back section into three to make the legs and tail.
Use the straws from both sides to make the back legs, bending
them at right angles to the body and tying each one round
with thread at the top, centre and foot. Use the top straws to
form the tail and plait it so that it stands up from the body. Tie
to secure and trim.

Divide the front straws into three. The outside straws on
each side are turned down to make the front legs and bound
as for the back ones. Turn the remaining straws up to form the
neck and tie at the base of the head. Separate two small
groups of top straws to make the horns and tie loosely out of
the way. Turn the head of the goat down and tie round the
muzzle to secure, incorporating a small bunch of heads of rye
under the chin to make a beard.

Plait the remaining two groups of top straws separately to
make the backward sloping horns. Some people insert a few
extra long straws into the neck when tying so that the horns
can be curled right over.

To complete, bind the goat with red ribbon in a criss-cross
fashion. *(Diag. 9.)*

*Diag. 8. Divide the bundle into three
equal parts.*

*Diag. 9. Bind the goat with red
ribbon.*

A Lavender Bottle

"Hot lavender", as Shakespeare called it, has been valued not only for its fragrance but also, since pagan times, for its medicinal properties. It was beloved of the Elizabethan house-wife in her stillroom where she extracted the oils and mixed them with powders and gentle salves in the fight for her family's health. It was used to perfume soaps and sweet confections and was placed in the linen chest to keep the moths at bay.

English lavender usually comes into full flower in late July when it is harvested and dried ready for selling. It still appears on market stalls and in the florists at the beginning of August for townspeople to buy. Forbidden by a London by-law from ringing bells and knocking on doors, the laven-der sellers of old used the Elizabethan street cry, "Lavender! Sweet lavender! Come buy my lavender!" until they were finally silenced by the war in 1914.

The lavender bottle takes its name from its shape and can be made from any uneven number of pairs of stalks, e.g. 7, 9 or 11 pairs. Pick it on a dry day when the flower is reaching full bloom.

Diag. 10.

Diag. 11.   Weave the ribbon through the stalks until all the flowers are hidden.

You will need:

14 heads of long-stemmed lavender
Lavender-coloured baby ribbon

To make:

Take the 14 heads of freshly-picked long-stemmed lavender and tie tightly together just beneath the heads using the baby ribbon. *(Diag. 10.)*

Bend each stem back over the flower heads so that all the stems are parallel and form a cage round the flowers. *(Diag. 11.)* Bring the ribbon through to the outside and weave in and out of the pairs of stalks until all the flowers are hidden. Tie

Diag. 12.

tightly at the top and finish with a bow. Trim the stalks. *(Diag. 12.)*

Apple Grannie

By mid-September the corn harvest is at an end. The "luck-sheaf" with an apple tucked inside was stored away for Christmas and the spring-born geese were let loose among the stubble in the fields to glean the stray grains and to fatten up for the Michaelmas Fair at the end of the month.

Apples, too, ripen this month and are harvested and stored in readiness for winter. They were long thought to have a magic of their own, and in Norse mythology were fed to the gods to forestall old age. Once used as a form of divination, a whole apple paring could be thrown over the right shoulder and whatever shape it formed as it landed was thought to be the initial of a future lover. The pips too were used in games of fortune and many young women placed them on the hot coals in the grate to test the fidelity of their husbands. Exploding pips meant a faithful husband.

The mountain people of the Southern Appalachians in North America have developed the art of making sweet potato and apple head dolls. Once a craft of the Seneca Indians of New York State, the dolls were fashioned for their children and it was believed they had the power to make wishes come true. The apples are peeled and carved, then dried very, very slowly and much of the fun comes from wondering just what the dried out faces will look like. The resulting characters are essentially old and grizzled, often called Apple Grannies.

You will need:

A large Golden Delicious apple – in good condition
Approx. 172 cm (68 in) wire
Small amount of Terylene wadding

Matching button thread for binding
Glue. Juice of a lemon. Salt
A little unspun sheep's wool for the hair
Scraps of fabric for clothes
Watercolour paints
Clear, matt varnish in an aerosol can – optional

To make:

Firstly prepare the apple which may take quite a long time before it becomes really hard, depending on the method of drying. Peel the apple very thinly and carve out the basic features of the eyes and nose, using a small pointed knife. Soak for 10 minutes in the juice of a lemon mixed with a dessertspoon of salt. Dab dry with kitchen paper. Place the apple on a wire rack in an oven with the pilot light on. *Do not* light the oven on a low setting to hasten the process or the apple will partially bake and the result will be a nasty mess rather than an apple head doll!

Alternatively, the apple can be dried on a wire rack over a radiator which is on a low setting. Cover with kitchen paper and turn every few days for even drying. Using this method, apples may take up to three weeks to become hard, but the slower and more gentle the process, the better. As they become easy to handle while drying, pinch and shape the features to accentuate them.

When completely hard, colour the cheeks and draw in the eyes and mouth using watercolour paint. Some people like to complete the head with a fine spray of matt varnish to keep out the air and help preserve the apple, but this is a modern innovation. Fluff up a small wad of unspun sheep's wool and glue onto the head to form the hair.

To make a wire armature for the body:

Cut the wire into two lengths – 100 cm (40 in) and 72 cm (28 in). Place the parallel wires with the centres together and

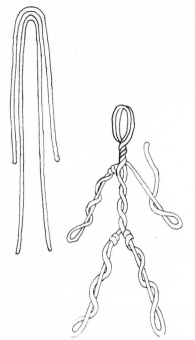

Diag. 13. Make a wire armature for the body.

bend in half. *(Diag. 13.)* Twist all four pieces together two or three times 4 cm (1½ in) from the top to make the neck. *(Diag. 13.)* Bend the two shorter lengths in half to make the arms and twist back towards the shoulder. Leave small loops at the ends for hands. Twist the two long pieces together for 10 cm (4 in) to form the body. Separate the wires to make the legs and repeat as for the arms. Wrap the body with the Terylene wadding and bind in place with button thread. Make the neck very firm and cover tightly with thread.

Make a small hole in the apple where the neck should be using a skewer. Twist the head section of the armature into a spike, cover with glue and push up into the dried apple head. Leave to set completely.

Traditionally Apple Grannies were dressed in old-fashioned mountain costume, rather like the women that made them. From your scraps of fabric make a long skirt trimmed with lace. Give her a matching poke bonnet and a plaid shawl to drape round her shoulders.

To make the bonnet:

Cut a circle of fabric 18 cm (7 in) in diameter and a rectangle 18 cm × 10 cm (7 in × 4 in). *(Diag. 14.)* Turn under and stitch down a tiny seam allowance all round the circle to neaten. Take a running stitch all round the edge and pull up into a cap that fits loosely on the doll's head. With right sides facing, fold the rectangle in half lengthways and stitch across the two short ends. Turn right side out. With right sides together, pin and stitch one long edge of the brim to the edge of the gathered cap. Turn under remaining seam allowance and hem down to the inside of the bonnet. Add two ribbons for tying.

As you get more familiar with making this kind of doll, you can try different ways of adding features. Little pieces of peel can be set into the raw apple before it is dried and grains of rice can be pushed into the mouth to make teeth. You might also try making hands and feet from a self-hardening clay.

Diag. 14.

Hallowe'en Lanterns

As the evenings grow shorter with the approach of autumn, the three days of Hallowtide are devoted to thoughts of the dead. This period marks, with the last of the harvest, the end of summer and beginning of winter. In the old Celtic calendar, the start of the new year was honoured at the feast of Samhain. The souls of the dead were thought to wander the earth at this time, celebrated in England on October 31st as All Hallows' Eve. As the harvest-end ceremonies and divination games were performed, ritual fires for the purification of the people and the land were once lit to overcome the powers of evil. These still blaze today, but the significance is lost and the accompanying rituals re-dedicated to Guy Fawkes and November 5th.

Candles also featured in the Hallowe'en processions as a guard against witchcraft and were lit for the dead and placed on the graves in the churchyard. In Ireland they burned in the windows to guide the spirits into where gifts of food, drink and tobacco were waiting on the table; the soul cakes still baked today were originally part of these offerings to the dead.

Most Hallowe'en parties sport an abundance of turnip lanterns and horrific masks which contribute to the fun, although the children playing are unaware of the origins of the ritual. Like the Hallowe'en Guisers of the north, the lanterns were a means of impersonating the returning dead and in so doing the bearers were afforded some protection against them. In parts of Wales and Somerset they are still hung on the gateposts to keep the house free from evil influence. These customs have taken root in America where the turnip lantern has been replaced by the pumpkin and groups of masked children still go round the houses playing "trick or treat".

Make a pumpkin lantern as a centrepiece for the party table. None of it is wasted, the flesh can be made into a pie and the seeds washed and dried and threaded into a necklace.

You will need:

Large pumpkin approx. 26 lb in weight
Sharp filleting knife. Tablespoon
Three nightlights
Greaseproof paper. Scissors

To make:

Slice off the top of the pumpkin, making a lid several inches

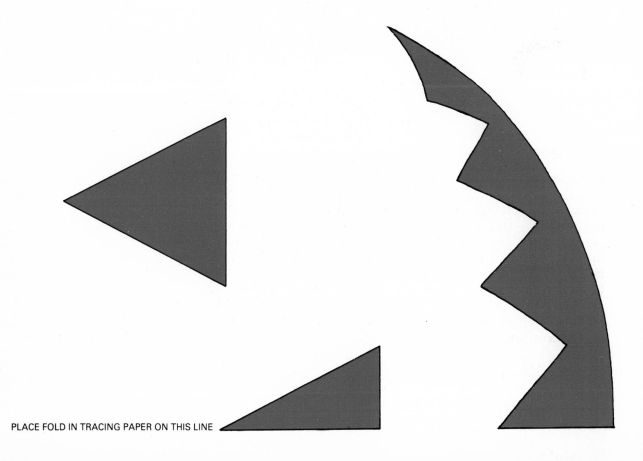

PLACE FOLD IN TRACING PAPER ON THIS LINE

across. Using the tablespoon, scoop out the seeds from the centre. Carefully scoop out some of the flesh leaving a shell of uniform thickness.

Trace the pattern *(Diag. 15.)* onto greaseproof paper and cut out the features. Position on the pumpkin and secure with Sellotape. Using the cut out areas as a guide, draw just inside the edges of the paper with a felt tip pen. Carve out the features using the filleting knife. Make sure the features are cut right through so that the candlelight can shine out of the holes. Place three or four nightlights inside the lantern and replace the lid.

If using a turnip, follow the same procedure but make two holes, one on either side of the head, and tie a string through each one to make a handle for carrying. The faces can be made more horrific by the addition of straggly hair glued to the sides of the lantern and perhaps a carrot nose impaled on a cocktail stick. How about a prize for the most inventive lantern?

Toffee Apples

In some places Hallowe'en is known as Crab Apple Night or Nut Crack Night, even Apple and Candle Night, all referring to the traditional games played on that evening with apples, nuts and fire. Ducking for apples is still played at Hallowe'en parties, the players with their hands clasped behind, plunging screwed up faces into a tub of water to try and catch a floating apple between their teeth. A less messy variation known as Snap Apple involves the players trying to bite the swinging fruit which has been suspended on a string. No Hallowe'en party is complete without toffee apples, so here is a simple recipe.

You will need:

4 firm apples
4 wooden skewers

225 g (8 oz) demerara sugar
2 tbsps butter
1 tbsp water
1 tbsp malt vinegar
Pinch of cream of tartar
Sheet of buttered paper
Heavy-bottomed saucepan. Sugar thermometer. Wooden spoon

To make:

Wash the apples but do not peel. Spear firmly onto the wooden skewers. Combine the sugar, butter and water in the saucepan and heat very gently, stirring all the time. When dissolved, add the vinegar. Increase the heat and boil the mixture until it reaches 170°C (325°F) on the sugar thermometer. As the mixture changes from a golden colour to brown, remove from the heat. Do not let it become very dark or it will be bitter. Dip the apples in the toffee, turning round gently so that the whole surface is covered. Stand with skewers upmost on buttered paper to set.

Masks and Disguises

Hand in hand with the pumpkins and games of the season go the Hallowe'en masks and disguises. Here is a pattern for a very simple mask which can be used as a base for paint or any other added decoration.

You will need:

Thin card. Scissors. Glue. Coloured paper or felt tip pens for decorating. String

To make:

Cut a rectangle of thin card 30 cm × 23 cm (12 in × 9 in). Mark centre top and bottom of the two long sides and round

Sun Mask. An Iroquois sun mask made from corn husks and still used in the winter ceremonies. There is evidence of worship of a Maize goddess throughout North and South America. The Iroquois Indians believe in a divine trinity of three sisters who represent the Spirits of the Corn, the Beans and the Squashes. They are known by one name only, De-o-ha'-ko, which means "Our Life" or "Our Supporters".

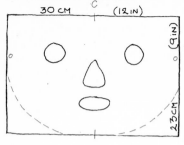

Diag. 16.   A basic mask to work on.

Diag. 17.   Paint the face like a tabby cat.

off the two bottom corners. Draw the features in position and cut them out. *(Diag. 16.)* This will form the base on which to make your design. Try the mask for size round your face and if too large, trim a small amount from the edges.

Decorate with coloured paints or stick on some cut out paper shapes. Make a witch's cat by slanting the eyes a little and trimming away the bottom of the mask to form jowls. Add long whiskers and pointed ears. *(Diag. 17.)*

To make ready for wearing, tie two lengths of string at the sides of the mask at eye level.

A string mask can be made quite easily based on the design of the Iroquois corn husk mask in the illustration on page 87.

You will need:

Thin card
Lots of string – in several thicknesses
Strong glue. Scissors

To make:

From thin card, make a basic mask as previously described. Make sure it fits snugly over the bridge of the nose.

Cut several long lengths of the finest string and plait together. The very thickest string can be unravelled and teased out to make hair and a beard.

Lay the mask out flat on some newspaper to work. Glue on the string, working on one part of the face at a time. First apply a good layer of glue to the area round the eyes.

Take a length of plaited string and coil it round each eye three or four times. Repeat round the mouth. Cut the thickest string into varying lengths, unravel and glue all round the edge of the mask in a straggly fringe. Glue more plaited string right round the face two or three times, covering the ends of the fringe and any bare patches of card on the cheeks.

The nose can be left open or covered. To make a nose, cut a small cone out of card and cover in single thickness string.

Glue in position over the nose hole. Leave the mask to dry completely before attempting to bend it to the face. Tie or stitch two cords at the sides of the mask at eye level.

You can also experiment with different beards and moustaches, or even change the expression on the face by altering the shapes of the features.

American illustrator Thomas Nast transformed St Nicholas into the jolly Santa we know today.

DECORATING THE HOME FOR CHRISTMAS

When the church authorities moved the celebration of the birth of Christ from January 6th to December 25th they were but drawing the thin veil of Christianity over an ancient fire festival celebrated by pagans as the Birthday of the Unconquered Sun. The winter solstice had long been a time for rejoicing. As the sun began its slow climb heavenward on December 21st, the shortest, darkest day of the year, fires were lit in anticipation of the return of light and warmth.

There is evidence to suggest that winter fire festivals were held in the ancient world in places as far apart as Rome and Babylon. The Roman Saturnalia, which raged for seven unruly days, began on December 17th and was closely followed by the January Kalends held in honour of the New Year. At the Saturnalia, master and servant exchanged roles in imitation of man's equality in the Golden Age of Saturn's reign. During the three days of the Kalends, debauchery and merriment gave way to gentler celebration, when evergreens festooned the houses and gifts were offered to all.

Similarly, our Scandinavian ancestors lit their fires in honour of the god Thor, at the Feast of JUUL. These Nordic customs and superstitions moved south across Europe with their invading armies and eventually became woven in with the Celtic belief in the sacredness of perpetual fire.

Even when Christianity took hold, it became obvious that these pagan celebrations were not to be forgotten, so in its wisdom the Church joined them all together as one new festival, complete with Christian meaning and ceremony. And so it is that we celebrate today a period of rejoicing at the coming of Christ which is underlaid with pagan symbolism and ritual.

A legacy of the Saturnalia was the Medieval Feast of Fools presided over by the Lord of Misrule. Once again master and servant exchanged places, while the elected Lord distributed paper crowns to be worn during the revels which were strung out from All Hallows' Eve until Twelfth Night.

Although in the 1600s Cromwell tried his utmost to banish Christmas, he only succeeded in driving it temporarily underground. Perhaps this was the beginning of the true family Christmas, for after that time most of the big, public gatherings ceased. However, many of the old traditions were kept alive by the Christmas "guisers", that same band of mummers found at Easter, whose lineage goes back a thousand years. The plays hardly altered but the prime intention was to collect charity for the poor, as light, in the form of St George, triumphed over darkness, the Turkish Knight. Battle wounds were healed by the doctor with his magic potions and Opliss Popliss Drops and, in more recent years, Father Christmas was introduced to compère the proceedings. A strange background to the serious business of collecting food and money for the less fortunate.

At the heart of the Christmas festivities and still surviving in parts of Europe, was the burning of the great Yule Log. With its accompanying rites, it was the domestic counterpart of those huge communal bonfires lit by the Norsemen at their mid-winter feast. Decorated with evergreens, it was brought into the house with great ceremony on Christmas Eve and a fire kindled in the open hearth, using a fragment of the previous year's Log. It burned throughout the twelve days of Christmas and when finally allowed to die, a charred piece was put aside to continue the cycle.

Each country has vested the Yule Log with the usual powers of fertility, and in recognition of this it was often strewn with corn and cider before lighting. The ashes, like the wax from the Yule Candle, were endowed with special powers to protect and heal and were scattered over the fields. Devon farmers replaced the traditional Log with an ashen faggot, which was made up in the farmyard and held together with nine bands of twisted hazel. As each band snapped in the flames, it was taken as a form of divination by the unmarried girls or a signal for more spiced ale and toasts by the men.

Of course, every child awaits with undisguised excitement the nocturnal visit of the jolly, white-bearded gift bringer. A figure of indeterminate pedigree, Father Christmas has several ancestors. In Norse legend, it was Odin's chariot which careered across the darkened skies as he showered presents on the children of northern lands. Christianity usurped him in favour of St Nicholas, a fourth-century bishop of Myra, whose feast day is December 6th. The old Father Christmas or Sir Christmas of the English mumming plays, had no religious background, the term "Father" being just a respectful form of address for an elderly man. Much later, when he became seen as the embodiment of the Christmas spirit and with the arrival of Santa Claus from America in the 1800s, the two became fused together.

Santa's modern appearance was largely due to an American illustrator, Thomas Nast, who transformed the rather saintly looking bishop into a jovial character complete with church-warden pipe and an armful of toys. His team of reindeer was also added in America, although Rudolph the Red Nosed Reindeer didn't make his début until 1939 with the publication of the song of that name. A sad and failed beast, Rudolph with his glowing nose was a figure of fun and ridicule, until Santa put it to good use and asked him to lead the team and light his sleigh through the night.

Following a huge nineteenth-century revival of Christmas festivities and before the true sentiments of charity and goodwill were swamped by commercialism, the Christmas tree became established as part of the English Yuletide scene. It crossed from Germany to England in the 1820s, but how long it was known in that country beforehand is uncertain. Various legends connect it with St Boniface in the eighth century, who replaced the sacred oak of Odin with a fir dedicated to the Holy Child. Much later, Martin Luther is credited with its introduction, although there is little evidence to support either story. Was it perhaps just a continuance of the age-old custom of decorating the house with evergreens at the winter feast, as a sign of continuing life?

By 1841, Prince Albert and Queen Victoria had introduced the candlelit tree to Windsor Castle. From then on it gained popularity and gradually replaced the far older Kissing Bough so beloved of the English. Traditionally decorated with fruits, gilded nuts and gingerbread, the tree acquired candles while still in Germany in the mid-1700s. It was topped by a Christ-child angel with golden hair, but this has since evolved into the less symbolic figure of the Christmas fairy.

In most countries Christmas has replaced Easter as the most important Christian festival of the year. Apart from its obvious religious significance, it is essentially a time of giving and sharing. I hope that by learning to make our own decorations and presents we can return to the traditional simplicity once found at that season.

CHRISTMAS CARDS

Cards arrived on the Christmas scene during Queen Victoria's reign and were intended to be sent by the penny post which was instituted in 1840. Although there are several claimants for the honour, it is thought that the first card was designed in 1843 by John Calcott Horsley for Henry Cole, founder of the Victoria and Albert Museum. It was sold for one shilling a copy at Felix Summerly's Treasure House in Bond Street. As improved printing techniques produced cheaper and more elaborate results and with the introduction of the halfpenny post, they became firmly established as an essential part of Christmas. The popular image of the robin redbreast on cards has remained constant as a symbol of life-giving fire at the time of the winter solstice.

There are so many different ways of making Christmas cards, but here are a few to start you off. Potato printing is suitable if you intend to mass-produce, whereas a jumping jack takes more time but could double as a card and present for someone special. Before beginning work, buy a packet of envelopes, then cut your cards so they will fit these when folded. Try and use quite stiff paper for all cards so they will stand up.

Potato Prints

You will need:

1 large potato
Sharp knife
Fine brush if adding detail
Saucer of poster paint – thickly mixed
Paper of choice – try coloured or textured as well as white

To make:

Cut several rectangles of paper and fold in half to make cards. Cut the potato in half. Cover the cut surface with paint and test to see if it is even by pressing onto a newspaper. If any areas of white show on the print, take a slice off the potato to level it up.

Mark the design onto the printing surface and very carefully cut all round with the sharp knife, until it stands out in relief. If carving letters remember to do them in reverse! *(Diag. 1.)* Dip into the paint and print onto the ready folded cards. When dry add any detail, using a fine watercolour brush.

You can repeat the block several times on one card, or use two or three different sized blocks, or perhaps add gold or silver glitter frost to the print.

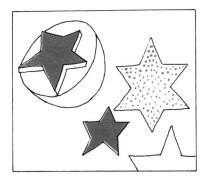

Diag. 1. *Try several shapes on one card.*

Diag. 2.

Thumb Prints

Press your thumb onto some very thinly spread oil paint or coloured ink, then press it onto a ready folded card. Don't overload with too much ink or the print will spread. Let it dry thoroughly, then add silly features with a pen or a fine paint brush. How about a cartoon robin or a reindeer? *(Diag. 2.)*

A Cracker Card – (this one will fit a standard envelope)

You will need:

Stiff paper
Felt tip pens or poster paint

To make:

Cut a rectangle of paper 40 cm × 9 cm (16 in × 3½ in). Fold into sections as in *Diag. 3*. Draw and paint a Christmas cracker on the front, taking the design right across the centre fold. Open up the card and continue the cracker on the inside of

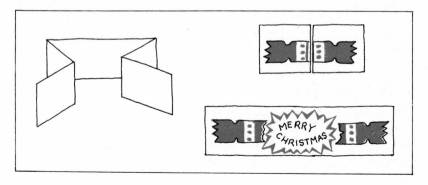

Diag. 3.   Fold the card into three sections.

each fold. Draw the edges jaggedly as if it had been pulled. Draw and paint the words "Merry Christmas" across the inside section of the card and enclose them in a coloured flash of red and yellow.

Snowflakes – (described so appropriately in the book of Job as "treasures of the snow")

The design in *Diag. 4.* can be used in several ways. Trace the whole quarter section of the snowflake onto a piece of folded tracing paper. Reverse the tracing to complete the design. Transfer to thin card and cut out, using a sharp handicraft knife. Use as a stencil by stippling paint through the cut out shape. Apply a water based paint (acrylic dries quickly) using a flat-ended brush. Spray-on snow can also look effective if the background colour is dark.

Diag. 4.

Alternatively, make a papercut. Cut a circle of fine, white paper, 10 cm (2 in) in diameter. Fold in half, then in half again, then once more, making eight segments. Trace the design from *Diag. 4.*, using the section between the dotted lines only. Transfer to the folded paper circle and cut out with sharp scissors. Open out the snowflake and glue onto a dark background.

This same shape can be made into a tree decoration. Cut several out of card, glue lightly both sides and dust with glitter. They can also be cut from heavyweight craft foil, which is double-sided and comes in very bright colours.

A Jumping Jack

These became very popular in France during the eighteenth century. Here is one in the shape of Father Christmas which would make a lovely present. Make it from a substantial card so that it will stand playing with.

You will need:

Strong white card
Tracing paper
4 split paper fasteners
1 curtain ring
Fine string or thick crochet cotton for stringing the figure
Large darning needle. Scissors
Poster or acrylic paint
Blob of cotton wool and glue (optional)

To make:

Trace the individual sections from *Diag. 5.* and transfer to white card. Cut out. Draw and paint in the features and then the costume on all five parts. Let them dry completely.

Using a large darning needle, make a hole in the centre of each marked hollow circle where the paper fasteners are to be put through. Insert a fastener into the hole and twist round a few times to enlarge. This will allow the limbs to move easily when strung. Make smaller holes where the black dots are marked for the strings.

Join all the parts together with fasteners, positioning the limbs behind the body and taking the fasteners through from the front to the back. Then string the figure as in *Diag. 6.* The arms and legs should hang down straight so that when the control string is pulled, they will move up and down.

To string the puppet, first attach a string to join the tops of the arms. Knot firmly to secure. Then attach one for the legs. These should be taut. Attach a third thread to the centre of the arm string and bring it down and join to the centre of the leg string. Tie a curtain ring to the end for easy pulling. Make a hole in the top of Santa's hat and tie on a thread for hanging. Finally, give him a cotton wool beard and snowy cuffs and boots if you like.

Diag. 5.   Trace the arms, legs and body separately.

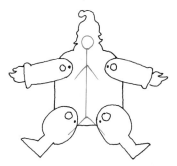

Diag. 6.   Tie the strings at the back of the figure.

The Advent Calendar

In the north of England it was customary for poor women to visit neighbours during Advent, bearing a box containing two little dolls, the Advent Images. These represented Christ and the Virgin Mary. Following an old tradition, the women collected alms and it was considered quite unlucky for a household not to have had a visit by Christmas Eve.

In Germany, this period has taken on even greater significance, with Advent wreaths and calendars to be found in most homes. First produced in about 1890, the calendars were used to introduce children to the twenty-four days of Advent, the period of preparation for Christ's coming. Some have pictures only, the more expensive have little gifts of charms and sweets hidden behind the windows in boxes. Opening one window each day can make the countdown to Christmas pass more quickly.

You will need:

Thin white card – 28 cm × 30 cm (11 in × 12 in)
Thick card the same size for backing
Pencil. Ruler. Glue. Handicraft knife. Acrylic or poster paints
Old Christmas cards
Small adhesive numbers – red or gold

To make:

Cut both pieces of card to size. Starting with the backing card, draw out a grid of 24 windows. (*Diag. 7.*) First pencil in the base line of the house, 5 cm (2 in) from the bottom of the card. Mark the centre. Measure and draw in the shape of the house. Within this shape fit the 24 windows. Each one is 2.5 cm (1 in) square and all are 1 cm (⅜ in) apart. Repeat exactly on the cover card.

Cut out small pictures and motifs from the old Christmas cards and stick one in each window on the backing card.

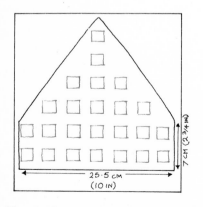

Diag. 7.   Draw a grid of 24 windows.

Draw in the house on the cover card. Give it a chimney and perhaps a picket fence or a snowman in the front garden. Put a deep band of snow all over the roof and porch and on top of the chimney. Cut out both cards to size.

Using a ruler and sharp handicraft knife, cut the top, bottom and centre of each window on the cover card, leaving both long sides as a hinge. *(Diag. 8.)*

Diag. 8. *Behind each window is a Christmas symbol.*

Open each of the windows in turn, bending the hinges back against a ruler to make a straight edge. Return to the closed position. Glue the two cards together, taking care not to get any adhesive on the backs of the windows.

Paint in the house and garden. When completely dry and using stick-on numbers or paint, number the windows from 1 to 24, starting at the top of the house. *(Diag. 9.)* You might like to experiment by doing a drawing of your own house and altering the 24 windows to fit.

An Advent Wreath and Calendar

Diag. 9.

You will need:

Thick wire or cane – two lengths of 102 cm (40 in)
Sprigs of evergreen, cut into short lengths (approx. 6 in or 10–15 cm)
Fine wire or buttonhole thread for binding
24 matchboxes
Wrapping paper – plain or striped looks best
Narrow ribbon in matching colour
24 small trinkets or sweets
Adhesive gold numbers 1–24
2.5 cm (1 in) width matching ribbon for hanging

To make:

Make both lengths of wire or cane into a circle 30 cm (12 in) in diameter. Bind together with sticky tape. Working round the

Diag. 10.   Number the boxes 1–24.

circle, bind the lengths of greenery onto the frame, using fine wire or buttonhole thread. Don't pad it too thickly or it will be too heavy.

Place a small toy or two or three wrapped sweets in each matchbox and make into a parcel. Leave one end of the wrapping paper free and tie round with narrow ribbon, leaving enough ribbon to attach the parcel to the wreath. Number all the boxes 1–24, using adhesive stickers. Tie them all round the wreath so that they hang at different lengths and suspend it from the ceiling by cord or wide ribbon. See page 27. *(Diag. 10.)*

DECORATING THE TREE

Tree decorations can be made very simply and don't have to be expensive. I found some sequin waste for sale by the yard in my local shop and used it to make flat stars and angels' wings. Do try and improvise when the recommended materials are not available.

Christmas Angel

This pattern can be made smaller or larger by changing the diameter of the outer circle and adjusting the body to fit. I made it from foil but you could cut it out of thin white card and decorate the wings with tiny motifs cut from silver paper doileys.

You will need:

Double-sided gold foil
Compass. Sharp handicraft knife. Hard pencil

To make:

Trace the pattern from *Diag. 11.* and transfer to double-sided gold foil, marking through the tracing with a hard pencil. Cut out along the solid lines. Using a sharp handicraft knife, carefully cut round the halo and top of the angel's head, following the dotted lines. Bend section A forward and cut out the edges of the sleeves. If using card, paint in the features. Curve the foil wings back a little from the body. Tie a fine thread at the top for hanging.

Angels from Fir Cones and Nuts

You will need:

Little wooden balls, 2 cm (¾ in) in diameter
Small larch cones or large hazelnuts
Stiff gold paper or card
Gold embroidery or lurex knitting thread
Strong glue. Scissors

To make:

For the body, snip the stalk off the larch cone and make the end flat. Glue a wooden ball to the cone at this point, for the head. Leave to dry completely.

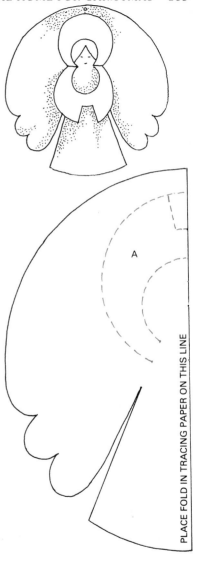

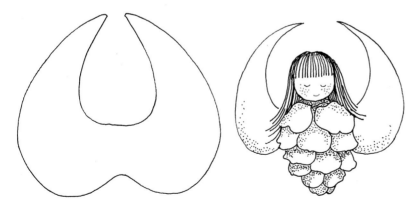

Diag. 12.   Make the wings from gold card.

Diag. 11.   Cut from double-sided foil.

PLACE FOLD IN TRACING PAPER ON THIS LINE

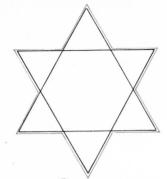

Diag. 13.   Make in several sizes and hang on the tree.

To make the hair, cut several strands of gold thread approx. 5 cm (2 in) in length. Tie together with a long thread, 1 cm (⅜ in) from one end. Do not trim but leave for hanging. Glue the hair to the head at the top and back, positioning the point where it is tied together at the top, centre of the ball. Bring the short ends forward to make a fringe and glue down. Draw in tiny features with paint or a felt tip pen.

Trace the wings from *Diag. 12.* and transfer to gold card. Cut out and glue in place at the centre back of the angel.

You can make these little angels in exactly the same way using hazelnuts in place of fir cones.

Stars

One of the universal symbols of Christmas, they can be hung in the window like the German Advent star, made into mobiles or put on the Christmas tree. Use double-sided foil for your tree decorations and they will pick up and reflect the light from the candles and fairy lights, making the whole tree shimmer.

To make a three-dimensional, six-pointed star, scale up the drawing in *Diag. 13.* and transfer to card. Cut out accurately and use as a template. Cut four pieces of double-sided foil, each one 9 cm (3½ in) square. Lay them in a stack, with gold surface to gold and green against green, so that when the star is opened out the colours will be seen alternately. Draw round your template with a hard pencil and cut out all four stars. Staple at the centre to hold and take a fine thread through the top points of the star for hanging. Open out. Make at least a dozen of these for a medium sized tree.

You can make a flat sided, six pointed star for the top of the tree by folding coloured paper or foil.

Using a protractor, draw an equilateral triangle with sides measuring 30 cm (12 in) in length. This will give a 15 cm (6 in) star. The angles at the corners should be 60°. Mark the centre of each side and using a ruler from these points find the centre

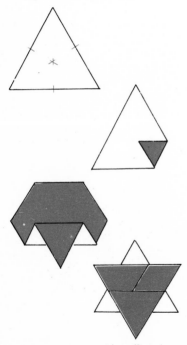

Diag. 14.   Use a folded star for the top of the tree.

of the triangle. *(Diag. 14.)* Cut out. Fold all three points of the triangle into the centre, making a hexagon. Turn over and fold each of the three sections again, taking the outer edges to the centre and turning out the points.

Folded stars look attractive made from a two-coloured foil.

Multi-pointed quill star

This star is made from two halves which are glued together.

You will need:

Double-sided coloured foil. Compass. Scissors. Glue and thread

To make:

Cut eight circles from double-sided foil, either in pairs of several colours or all from one colour. Cut two measuring 12 cm (5 in) in diameter, two 10 cm (4 in), two 8 cm (3 in) and two 6 cm (2½ in). Draw a second circle in the centre of each one, 3 cm (1¼ in) in diameter. Fold each circle in half, then in half again, and then once more. Open out and cut along the crease lines to the edge of the inner circle, making eight segments. *(Diag. 15.)*

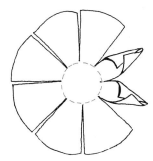

Diag. 15. *Fold and cut the circle into eight segments.*

Roll each segment into a cone and secure with a dab of glue. If you find shaping the cones difficult, curl them round the handle of a small watercolour brush. Repeat with remaining circles, until they have all been made into star shapes.

Thread four of the stars together, starting with a small one for the middle. Secure the thread with a tiny bead or sequin to prevent it pulling through the foil. Put a dab of glue at each centre, then pull up the thread, positioning the points of each star between those of the preceding one. *(Diag. 16.)* Repeat with remaining four sections and leave the thread in place for hanging. Glue both halves together at centre back.

Try creating your own shapes by altering the sizes of the

Diag. 16. *Join four sections to make a star.*

circles and by threading together in different ways. The quill stars in the photograph on page 59 are all made from the same pattern but are threaded differently. The two halves when made up, can also be used singly.

GIVING PRESENTS

The giving of gifts at the winter solstice has a long tradition. The Romans gave evergreen branches from the grove of the goddess Strenia as seasonal offerings to the emperor at the January Kalends, and during his own reign Caligula made this an order. In time they came to expect more; "honeyed things" for a New Year of peace, gold and silver to ensure continued wealth. Norsemen looked to Odin, who rode the midnight sky dispensing presents to the good and punishment to the bad, before being banished by the Christian Church in favour of St Nicholas. But present giving continues, assuming great importance over a long period of time, starting with the Eve of St Nicholas on December 5th right through Christmas to the Eve of Epiphany on January 5th, depending on the traditions of the country. Perhaps the dark haired First Footers of Scotland are continuing that long tradition with their offerings of bread and coal to welcome the New Year.

Paper Hearts and Cones

In Denmark small presents are hung on the Christmas tree in little paper hearts and cones.

You will need:

Coloured paper and glue (or Sellotape)

To make a heart:

Cut two strips of paper 26 cm × 10 cm (10 in × 4 in) in

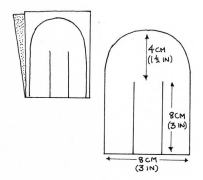

Diag. 17.   Cut two shapes in contrasting colours.

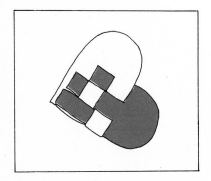

Diag. 18.   Weave the two sections together.

contrasting colours. Fold in half widthways. Using *Diag. 17.* as a guide, draw out the two halves of the heart, keeping the fold of the paper at the bottom. Cut out, then cut two slits on each section as shown by the black lines, giving three strips of equal width.

Hold the white section in the left hand, and the red section in the right, with the strips pointing upwards. Beginning with the two inner strips of each section, weave the two sections together, slotting each strip in turn through alternate loops as you work across the heart. *(Diag. 18.)*

The finished heart will open out like a little basket. Cut a strip of paper 20 cm (8 in) long for a handle and glue or tape in place inside the basket. *(Diag. 19.)* These can also look very attractive made from coloured felt.

Diag. 19.   Open out into a basket.

To make a cone:

Cut a piece of brightly coloured paper 13 cm (5 in) square, and a strip 1.5 cm × 20 cm (⅝ in × 8 in) for the handle. Glue or tape the handle at one corner of the square. Glue along one front edge and join the other edge to it. *(Diag. 20.)* Keep plain or decorate.

Boxes

Small, odd-shaped presents are often difficult to wrap so here are a few boxes to solve the problem. The basic cube is the easiest to make and can be given a new look each time by cutting it from a different coloured card. Alternatively, it can be made from plain card and decorated with anything you fancy.

Boxes can be made from cardboard of varying weights. Use card the thickness of cereal packets for small ones. Coloured foil board is ideal and doesn't have to be scored along the seams, only bent over a ruler to give a firm, straight edge.

Diag. 20.   Make squares of paper into cones.

If scaling up the basic pattern to enlarge, make the box from heavier card and score along the seams very lightly, through the top surface of the paper only so it will bend accurately. Mark the lines in pencil first and always use a steel ruler and a sharp handicraft knife or scalpel when cutting. Stick the seams with a clear adhesive and for very heavy card use a PVA wood glue.

One piece cube

Draw out *Diag. 21.* onto card of choice, making all sides 5 cm (2 in) square. These measurements must be accurate, so check with a protractor that the angles at the corners are 90°. Cut out along the solid lines. If using a card that needs to be scored, do so on the right side of the card, along the dotted lines. If the box is cut from lightweight card, fold each seam in turn up against the edge of the ruler, then rub down with your thumb nail placed over a piece of protective paper. Glue A to B and leave to dry. Fold in the remaining tabs and the lid and base at top and bottom.

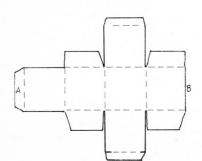

Diag. 21.   Fold along the dotted lines.

Box with a handle

Draw out *Diag. 22.* onto card. (I used gold foil board.) All sides of the box are 7.5 cm (3 in) square. Use a compass to draw the handles. Draw two semicircles from the centre point of the lid, one inside the other. The outer circle has a radius of 2.5 cm (1 in) and the handle 1 cm (½ in) thick. The slots in the remaining two sections of the lid are 5 cm (2 in) long and are positioned vertically 1 cm (½ in) from the point. Cut out as before, taking great care round the handles. Score or bend along the dotted lines. Glue A to B and leave to dry. Fold in the two tabs and base of the box. Fold over and bring together the two handles at the top of the box. Hold in place with the two slotted sections of the lid.

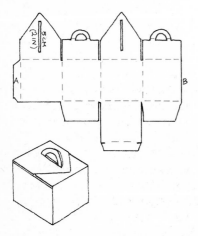

Diag. 22.

A Pyramid

The size given is suitable for holding a piece of jewellery. Make from a heavy card so it will close neatly.

Using a protractor, draw an equilateral triangle with sides measuring 18 cm (7 in) in length. The angle at the corners should be 60°. Mark the centre of each side and join these points together to make a smaller triangle within the first. (*Diag. 23.*) Cut out along the solid lines and score lightly along the dotted ones. Make a small hole at all three points of the large triangle and thread with a coloured cord to close.

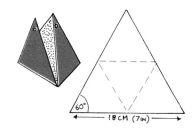

Diag. 23.   All the boxes can be made in different sizes.

Bows

A decorative bow can give your boxes and parcels a professional finish. Make them from paper gift ribbon which can be moistened and pressed together to secure, and choose a colour that is complementary to your box. Black and gold striped ribbon can look dramatic against a silver foil box, whereas the same box pattern made up in red card could be tied with a white bow printed with red hearts. Use the patterned ones for simple bows and the plain colours for the more complicated designs. Do remember that they don't always have to sit glued to the centre of a box; try a rectangle with a bow at one end or at the corner. The most common width used is 2 cm (¾ in).

To make a figure of eight bow, cut a length of ribbon approximately 60 cm (24 in) in length. Loop into a figure of eight at one end and secure at the centre. Repeat twice with the remaining ribbon, making each figure of eight slightly smaller than the previous one. Turn the end piece underneath to secure. (*Diag. 24.*)

To make a star rosette, cut two lengths of ribbon approximately 40 cm (16 in) in length. Loop half the first length of ribbon into a figure of eight, giving each loop a half twist and

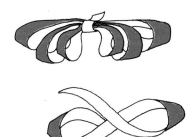

Diag. 24.   A figure of eight.

Diag. 25. *A star rosette.*

moistening at the centre to hold. Repeat with the remaining half, but positioning the loops at right angles to the first two. Do the same with the second length. Fix one in place diagonally on top of the other and secure at centre. *(Diag. 25.)*

PAPER CHAINS AND STREAMERS

Branches of evergreen, with their clusters of red and white berries, were once the main form of decoration at Christmas time. To our ancestors they symbolised continuing life, when all other plants had died and gone underground. Superstition dictates that they must not be brought into the house before Christmas Eve or taken down and burnt until Twelfth Night, or bad luck will follow. Today we still garland our homes with trails of holly and ivy, but now they are mixed with paper decorations made popular in the nineteenth century.

Shop-bought paper chains and streamers are often very dull, but they can so easily be made at home from any scraps of paper, preferably coloured on both sides. Collect together any shiny covers, jazzy paper bags, wrapping paper, gummed squares, anything bright or glossy. Try not to use fragile papers or the chains will break at a weak link.

Cut the paper into strips approximately 25 cm × 2.5 cm (10 in × 1 in) and glue together as interlocking links. Alternatively, make the strips into separate links, press flat, then join together at the centre of each side with a dab of glue. *(Diag. 26.)* Lastly, glue a small square of card to the end two links. This will give a firm base for the pins when hanging so that the chains are less likely to rip away and fall. Chains made in this way can be folded flat and stored for next year.

Streamers are made from crêpe paper. To make a two-colour twist, cut several 7 cm (2½ in) wide bands across the folded length of paper. This will give streamers of approximately 3 m (10 ft) in length. Unfold and join two lengths of different colours together by taking a line of machine stitching

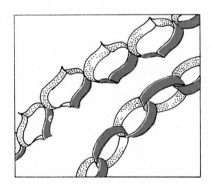

Diag. 26. *Paper chains can be linked or glued together.*

down the centre of the strips. Separate and frill the edges of each strip by stretching very gently or fringing with scissors. Twist the streamers when hanging.

Delicate tissue paper garlands are slightly more tricky to make but worth the effort. Cut several strips of coloured tissue paper 9 cm (3¼ in) wide and the length of the sheet of paper. Fold lengthways into a zig-zag of three, taking the sides to the centre and giving a strip 3 cm (1¼ in) wide. *(Diag. 27.)*

Make 2 cm (¾ in) deep cuts all along one edge, at 2 cm (¾ in) intervals. Turn and repeat along the other edge, positioning this second row of cuts between the first. Carefully open out and glue three or four sections together to make a long garland. Add small cardboard tabs at either end as previously described.

Shorter, free-hanging streamers can be made up with coloured craft foil and beads. Arrange them across a window or suspend from the ceiling near the chimney, where they can turn freely in the warm air.

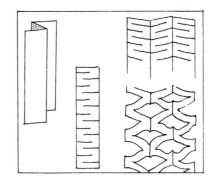

Diag. 27. Use tissue paper to make lacy garlands.

You will need:

Double-sided foil
Brightly coloured or metallic beads 1 cm (⅜ in) in diameter
Needle and button thread. Compass. Scissors

To make:

Cut a selection of discs from double-sided foil, 2.5 cm (1 in), 4 cm (1½ in), and 5.5 cm (2¼ in) in diameter. Using about 1 m (1 yd) of strong cotton, thread together, alternating the different sized discs and spacing them out with two or three coloured beads *(Diag. 28.)* Knot to secure and leave a loop for hanging.

If you have made little paper hearts (p.106) for the tree you might like to continue the theme.

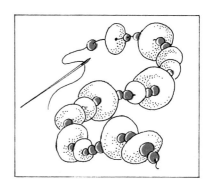

Diag. 28. Join the coloured foil and beads with thread.

Diag. 29.   Make from card that is coloured on both sides.

You will need:

Thin red card, coloured both sides
Strong, fine thread in matching colour
Sharp handicraft knife
Glue. Tracing paper

To make:

Trace the drawing from *Diag. 29*. and transfer to card. Using a sharp blade, cut out very carefully. Remove the four hearts from the centre of the shape, cutting along the dotted lines. Make three or four of these, depending on the length of streamer required. Lay out all the shapes in a row, about 1 cm (½ in) apart. Put a dab of glue along the centre of each shape and lay a length of thread over the top. Leave enough thread to make a loop at one end. Let the glue set completely before hanging.

Crackers

When confectioner Tom Smith returned from a business trip to France in 1840, he brought with him a selection of "bon-bons" – little sugared almonds wrapped in double-ended twists of coloured paper. To the English this was a novel way of buying sweets at Christmas, as they had previously been sold unwrapped. He began producing his own bonbons and added charms and toys and little "kiss mottoes" to exploit the seasonal angle. Eventually he hit on the idea of adding a bang and after much experimenting came up with a saltpetre friction strip which was designed to create a small explosion as the bonbon was pulled in two. Crackers were born!

Sadly, many of the shop-bought crackers are a disappointment. They are expensive and the contents often cheap and nasty. Try making your own, not just for Christmas, but for any family celebration. All the materials are easily found and the bangers or snaps can be bought from specialist suppliers. Ask father to write some of his dreadful puns for the inside!

The outer casings are usually made from crêpe paper, but other fancy papers will do as long as they tear easily. Test by cutting an oblong with the grain of the paper running lengthwise, roll into a cylinder and pull in two. If it tears with ease then it is suitable for cracker making.

You will need:

Crêpe paper – in colour of choice

Lining paper – must be thin, airmail paper or copy paper for typing will do

Thin card for the centre tube – cut from empty cereal packets or tissue boxes

2 former tubes – must be firm in order to shape the cracker while working, approximately 12.5 cm (5 in) and 25 cm (10 in) × 4 cm (1½ in) in diameter. The inside roll from kitchen foil or a plastic water pipe will do

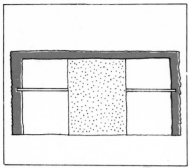

Diag. 30.   Lay the papers and card on top of each other.

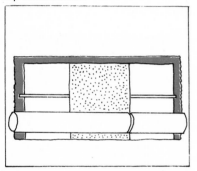

Diag. 31.   Put the formers in position.

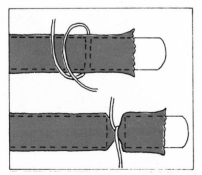

Diag. 32.   Pull the string tight to shape the end of the cracker.

Fillings – anything you choose, paper hats, mottoes, tiny presents
Snaps – from specialist suppliers
Clear adhesive. Thin string for shaping. Ruler. Scissors

To make:

For each cracker cut one piece of crêpe paper with the grain lengthwise, 30 cm × 16 cm (12 in × 6¼ in), one piece of lining paper 28 cm × 15 cm (11 in × 6 in) and one cardboard stiffener 11.5 cm × 15 cm (4½ in × 6 in). Frill the short ends of the crêpe paper by stretching gently.

Lay the crêpe paper out horizontally, then the lining 1 cm (¼ in) down from the top edge. Place a snap and a motto in the centre and place the stiffening card vertically on top. *(Diag. 30.)* Squeeze a line of glue along the top edges of the papers. Lay the two formers in position, the small one on the right and the butted up edges where they meet directly over the right hand edge of the stiffening card. *(Diag. 31.)* Roll up tightly into a tube and smooth down the glued edge so it holds.

Tie a length of string round the back leg of your work table and bring it over the tabletop to your work area. Place the rolled cracker over the string, and leaving the large former tube in position, ease out the small former from the right hand side exactly 3.5 cm (1⅜ in). Wind the string round the cracker centrally between the formers and pull up tightly to close one end of the cracker. *(Diag. 32.)* Push the small tube back into position against the larger one to shape the end of the cracker, then remove completely. Untie the string but do not let the large former move.

Drop a little gift and a paper hat down the tube into the cracker. Place with the open end to the right, ease out the remaining former by 3.5 cm (1⅜ in) and repeat as before.

To decorate, glue bands of wide gold cake trim on the centre section and at both ends. Add a satin bow to the middle, or glue on bands of fancy braids or paper lace. Shapes cut from silver and gold doileys look pretty.

To make a frill, cut one piece of crêpe paper 9 cm × 23 cm (3½ in × 9 in), with the grain running parallel to the short ends of the paper. Frill the long edges by stretching gently. Fold over lengthways making two frills 5 cm (2 in) and 4 cm (1½ in) in depth. (*Diag. 33.*) Place a length of strong thread or crochet cotton along the fold, gather up the paper and tie round the gathered part of the cracker at the back. Knot and trim the thread. Repeat for other end. (*Diag. 34.*)

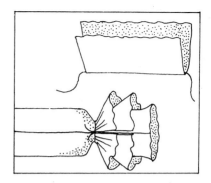

Diag. 33. Add a separate frill in a contrasting colour.

The Christmas Stocking

Dutch children leave their shoes in the hearth on December 5th in anticipation of a visit from St Nicholas. The good bishop will exchange their offerings of straw and carrots left there for his horse, for little sweets and gingerbread. In France a glass of water is put with the shoes to refresh Father Christmas on his travels. English children hang up the Christmas stocking on Christmas Eve, either from the mantelpiece or at the end of the bed.

The real St Nicholas was a wealthy man and had a reputation for spreading his money among the poor. Legend has it that he gave a bag of gold coins to a poor peasant about to sell his three daughters into slavery. Liking to remain anonymous, he tossed the gold through the open window and it landed in a stocking hung up by the fire to dry. This is how the custom of hanging up the Christmas stocking originated.

The contents have their own tradition. A rosy apple in the toe for good health, an orange in the heel for luxury, for until this century they were rare and expensive. A mint fresh penny for wealth, sometimes a bag of chocolate coins wrapped in gold foil to commemorate St Nicholas. Nuts, salt, and until quite recently, a lump of coal as a symbol of warmth for the coming year.

Diag. 34.

Every Christmas stocking must contain an apple, an orange and a bright new penny.

Make this stocking from bright red felt and use iron-on appliqué shapes to decorate.

You will need:

Dressmakers pattern paper
Red felt – 2 pieces 55 cm × 33 cm (22 in × 13 in)
White felt or short pile, fur fabric trim – 37 cm × 7 cm (14½ in × 3 in)
Scraps of coloured felt for appliqué shapes
Double-sided, iron-on bonding web

To make:

Scale up the pattern from *Diag. 35.* and draw out onto dressmakers pattern paper. Cut out. Using the pattern as a guide, cut two stocking pieces from red felt. Trace any of the shapes from *Diag. 36.* and transfer to the paper side of the adhesive bonding web. Cut out roughly. Place the adhesive side on to the pieces of coloured felt and iron in place. Leave to cool.

Cut out all the shapes. Peel off the paper backings and arrange the cut out shapes on one of the felt stocking pieces. Iron on using a damp cloth. Leave to cool completely before moving. You will find it easier to iron one shape at a time rather than the whole design. Add any extra shapes you fancy to the design using the same method.

Pin the two pieces of the stocking together and machine all round the sides and foot, using a matching thread and giving a 5 mm (³⁄₁₆ in) seam allowance. This will make a decorative edging as felt does not fray and needs no turning. Make the white felt into a band by stitching the two short ends together. Turn and slip over the top of the stocking. Line up the seams at the back and stitch in place around the top of the leg. Make a loop from a strip of felt 30 cm (12 in) in length and attach on the inside over the back seam.

If making the stocking from any fabric other than felt, allow

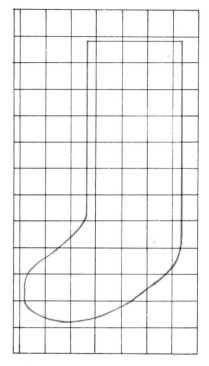

Diag. 35.   Draw out the stocking onto dressmaker's paper.

Diag. 36. Cut the shapes from coloured felt.

Diag. 37. Knitted and felt Christmas stockings.

a 1.5 cm (½ in) seam allowance all round the pattern when cutting out. Iron on the appliqué shapes to the right side of one of the pieces before making up. Pin the two pieces together with right sides facing, and machine all round the sides and foot. Clip on the curves and turn to right side. Turn over the edge at the top of the leg to the right side and machine down. Add the cuff as described above. *(Diag. 37.)*

SPICED BISCUITS AND GINGERBREAD

For centuries spiced cakes and biscuits have been baked all over Europe at Christmas time. They were often in the shape of oxen and pigs. Wreaths which represent the completed year are traditional, often with a space for a central candle. Sometimes they were baked in the shape of the Christ figure. All are a mixture of the usual symbolic sacrificial and Christian emblems found in many cultures. In Holland and Germany in particular, special wooden biscuit forms are used for shaping spiced biscuits into intricate designs. The dough is pressed into the floured mould, then turned out onto a baking sheet and cooked in the usual way.

Dutch Speculaas

These can be made a week or two before Christmas and will stay quite fresh in an airtight tin. If made into traditional rings, they can be threaded with ribbon and hung on the tree on Christmas Eve. The ingredients given will make approximately 30 biscuits using a 6 cm (2½ in) diameter cutter.

Ingredients:

150 g (6 oz) plain flour
¼ level tsp baking powder
Pinch of salt
75 g (3 oz) butter
75 g (3 oz) barbados sugar

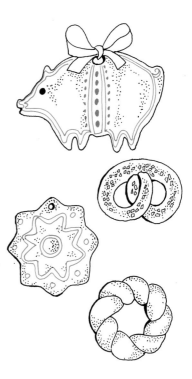

Diag. 38. Pipe round the shapes with icing.

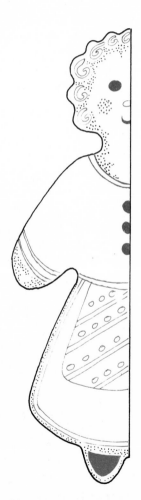

Diag. 39.　A gingerbread woman.

1½ level tsps mixed spice
1 egg yolk
1–2 tbsps milk
50 g (2 oz) flaked almonds
Decoration of choice. I use royal icing for piping

To make:

Sift the flour, salt and baking powder into a mixing bowl and rub in the butter. Stir in the sugar, spice and almonds. Add the egg yolk and a little milk if necessary and knead to a soft dough. Wrap the dough in a piece of foil and leave to rest for at least an hour in a cool place.

Grease one or two baking sheets. Dust working surface with flour and roll out the dough to a thickness of ½ cm (¼ in). Cut into figures or fluted rings, or moons and stars using biscuit cutters. If the shapes are to be hung on the tree, make a small hole before baking in the top of the biscuit using a skewer. Bake for 15–20 minutes in a moderate oven – 175°C (350°F), gas mark 4. Cool on a wire tray. Only use piped royal icing when biscuits are completely cool. *(Diag. 38.)*

Gingerbread Figures

Ginger was introduced to Europe by the Romans who brought it over from their African colonies. It became a favourite of English cooks who sprinkled it generously into their cakes and biscuits. In Elizabethan days, gingerbread was gilded, often with cloves or tiny box leaves dipped in gold and laid on in heraldic designs.

No German Christmas would be complete without its decorated gingerbread figures or a gingerbread witch's house, made from sweets, biscuits and icing sugar snow. Use this recipe to make figures for the tree. Trace the patterns given in *Diags. 39. and 40.* and transfer to card and use as a template when cutting out the dough. If you want to design your own shapes, remember to keep the outline simple so they are easy to cut out with a knife. You can always go to town on the decorating.

Ingredients:

200 g (7 oz) plain flour
1 level tsp baking powder
½ level tsp bicarbonate of soda
2 level tsps ground ginger
75 g (3 oz) butter
75 g (3 oz) soft brown sugar
30 ml (2 tbsps) golden syrup
Currants or tiny sweets for eyes and buttons. Alternatively, roll little pieces of gingerbread into features or if you happen to be icing the Christmas cake at the same time you could fill in the clothes with coloured icing

To make:

Pre-heat oven to 200°C (400°F), gas mark 6. Measure the butter, sugar and syrup into a saucepan and melt over a low heat. Stir until completely melted but not hot. Sift all the dry ingredients into a mixing bowl, then add the melted mixture to this. Mix into a dough using a wooden spoon. Turn onto a floured surface and knead. Allow to cool for a few minutes and to firm up.

Roll out to a thickness of 6 mm (¼ in). Cut out using your cardboard templates or biscuit cutters. Lay on a greased baking sheet and add currants for eyes. If you are going to use any other decoration add after baking, when completely cold.

Bake in batches in the centre of the oven for 10–15 minutes. Allow to cool on the baking sheet for a minute to firm up, then transfer to a wire cooling tray.

If using icing for clothes and features small amounts can be coloured with a few drops of edible food colouring.

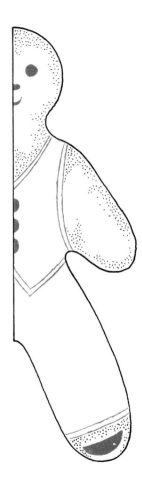

Diag. 40.   A gingerbread man.

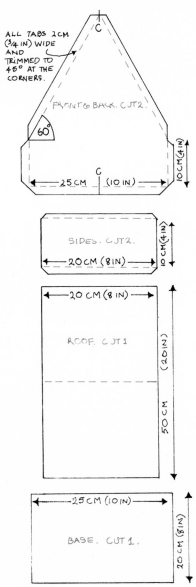

ALL TABS 2CM
(3/4 IN) WIDE
AND
TRIMMED TO
45° AT THE
CORNERS.

FRONT & BACK. CUT 2.

60°

25CM (10 IN)

10 CM (4 IN)

SIDES. CUT 2.
20CM (8 IN)
10 CM (4 IN)

20 CM (8 IN)

ROOF. CUT 1

50 CM (20 IN)

25 CM (10 IN)

BASE. CUT 1.

20 CM (8 IN)

Diag. 41.
Make the house from stiff white card.

Gingerbread House

A Hansel and Gretel house (see photograph on p. 75) can be made from sections of baked gingerbread glued together with icing, or a more decorative version made from lebkuchen and sweets on a cardboard base. It can then gradually be eaten up over the Christmas holiday.

You will need:

Thick white card
Metal ruler, sharp handicraft knife and glue
Icing sugar – approx. 2-3 packets
Selection of small biscuits, sweets, chocolate buttons, cake decorations, wafers and lebkuchen. Biscuits with jam-filled squares can be used for windows and any slim biscuit, round or square for roofing tiles. A slab of cake will do for the chimney
Marzipan and food colouring for modelling the garden if you are feeling adventurous

To make:

Scale up *Diag. 41.* and draw onto stiff, white card. Cut out along the solid lines, using a sharp blade. Score very lightly on the right side along the dotted lines and bend the tabs back ready for gluing. Glue the two sides of the house to the front and back sections, keeping the tabs inside. Leave to dry. Turn the bottom tabs under and glue the four walls to the base. Add the roof. Leave the house to dry completely for several hours before attempting to add the decoration or the walls may shift with the weight of the icing.

Before beginning work, sort out the biscuits and sweets and decide which ones you are going to use for the walls and roof. Reserve the very smallest for decorating round the door and window and cut a biscuit into an Advent star for the apex of the roof.

Mix up a bowl of stiff royal icing, following the manufacturer's instructions, but not too large an amount or it will set before it can be used up and will be wasted. Keep water and extra icing sugar at hand to adjust the consistency if necessary.

Starting at the back of the house and working on one section at a time, apply the decoration. Using a palette knife or spatula, cover the wall roughly with icing in a thin layer. Working from the base upwards towards the roof, press the biscuits into the icing while it is still soft. Repeat for the remaining three walls and use whole biscuits for windows and a door on the front section.

When set, repeat the process for the roof. Make a chimney on one side, cutting the biscuits or cake to fit the angle of the slope. Work from the edge of the roof up towards the ridge and let the tiles overhang a little at the front edge. You may be able to push the biscuits into the icing at an angle so they overlap like real roofing tiles. Decorate round the windows with the tiniest sweets.

Finally, make icicles to hang from the edge of the roof and chimney by dribbling soft icing off a spoon. Stand the finished house on a flat plate or a cake base. Roughly ice the ground at the base of the house, and make a little path and garden using small sweets and cake decorations.

List of suppliers all doing mail order

All candlemaking equipment: Candle Makers Supplies
28 Blythe Road
London W14 0HA

Double-sided craft foil: Westwood Stationery Ltd
54/58 Park Royal Road
London NW10 7JF

Anchor embroidery threads: Riess Wools
242–243 High Holborn
London WC1V 7DZ

A further list of mail order stockists of
Anchor embroidery threads is available from:
J & P Coats (UK) Ltd
Domestic Marketing Division
39 Durham Street
Glasgow G41 1BS

Coloured papers, boards and art materials:
Paperchase
213 Tottenham Court Road
London W1P 9AF

Arts & Graphics
4 West End
Redruth
Cornwall TR15 2RZ

Complete cracker kits: Stoneleigh Mail Order Co.
91 Prince Avenue
Southend-on-Sea
Essex

THE DIABETES HANDBOOK
Non-insulin Dependent
Diabetes

THE DIABETES HANDBOOK
Non-insulin Dependent Diabetes

Dr John L. Day M.D.,F.R.C.P.

Chairman of the BDA Education Advisory Committee

THORSONS PUBLISHING GROUP

Published in collaboration with
The British Diabetic Association
10 Queen Anne Street, London W1M 0BD

First published 1986

British Library Cataloguing in Publication Data

Day, John L.
  The diabetes handbook.
  Non-insulin dependent diabetes
  1. Diabetes — Treatment   2. Self-care,
  Health
  I. Title   II. British Diabetic Association
  616.4'6206   RC660

  ISBN 0-7225-1369-0

Printed and bound in Singapore

10 9 8 7 6 5 4 3

Contents

Foreword

Today people with diabetes can lead full and active lives and expect to be as healthy as people without diabetes. However, to enjoy good health with diabetes demands self-discipline, understanding and knowledge. Nobody can be expected to follow rules and recommendations without a clear explanation of the reasons for doing so.

So it is a pleasure to welcome this new British Diabetic Association Handbook. It is comprehensive and thoroughly up-to-date. It contains all the essential information.

The Handbook has been prepared by experts in the field. It is clearly and sympathetically written, copiously illustrated and well designed, so that even the most complex aspects of diabetes and its control are easy to understand. It is invaluable as a reference book and as an easy to follow practical guide to good diabetic control. Nobody with diabetes should be without it.

Sir Harry Secombe CBE

Introduction

The correct name for diabetes is diabetes mellitus. 'Diabetes' is derived from a Greek word meaning syphon, and 'mellitus' refers to the characteristic sweetness of the urine of people with diabetes. This title describes one of the most important features of the disease — the passage of very large amounts of sweet urine.

Diabetes is very common. In the UK there are more than 600,000 people with diabetes, of whom over 30,000 are children; world-wide there are over 30 million.

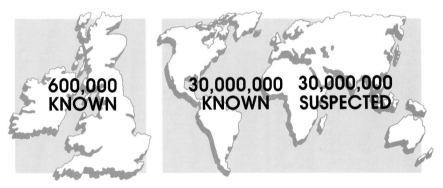

Fig. 1.1
The estimated numbers of people with diabetes.

Diabetes has been known to physicians for thousands of years, one of the first references to it being in the Ebers Papyrus (Fig. 1.2) written in Egypt in 1500 BC. It is also referred to in ancient Indian, Roman, Japanese and Chinese writings. However, it was not until the last century that any significant advance was made in understanding the nature of diabetes, or in developing an effective form of treatment. The first major breakthrough came in 1889, when two German scientists discovered that the removal of the pancreas, a large gland in the abdomen, gave rise to diabetes. About this time, it was also discovered that damage to specific cells in the

Fig. 1.2
The Ebers Papyrus.

Written about 1500 BC, this is one of the earliest documents describing the treatment of diabetes. The treatment is called "A medicine to drive away the passing of too much urine . . ." and included a mixture of bones, wheat grains, fresh grits, green lead, earth and water. These ingredients the user should "let stand moist, strain it, take it for four days."

The Payprus, measuring over 20 metres long and 30 centimetres wide, was found in a grave in Thebes in Egypt, in 1862.

pancreas, called islets of Langerhans, produced certain forms of diabetes. But it was not until 1921 that two Canadians, Frederick Banting and Charles Best (Fig. 1.3) made their famous discovery of insulin.

Fig. 1.3
Banting and Best.
Frederick Banting and Charles Best, whose research led to the isolation of insulin. The photograph shows them with their famous dog, Marjorie, which was kept alive by insulin after her pancreas had been removed.

Modern treatment enables many thousands of people with diabetes to achieve complete, fruitful, healthy lives and to fulfil their ambitions in all walks of life. Treatment is a bar to very few jobs. People with diabetes are found amongst our most successful actors, actresses, entertainers, politicians, first-class footballers, sportsmen and sportswomen competing at the highest level, and in all the professions; all of these bear witness to the fact that effective treatment can be combined with the highest achievements.

What is diabetes?

In simple terms, diabetes is a disorder in which the body is unable to control the amount of sugar in the blood, because the mechanism which converts sugar to energy is no longer functioning properly. This leads to an abnormally high level of sugar in the blood, which gives rise to a variety of symptoms. If the sugar levels are uncontrolled over several years, it may damage various tissues of the body. Therefore, the treatment of diabetes is designed not only to reverse any symptoms you might have at the beginning, but also to prevent any serious problems developing later.

How does diabetes develop?

Normally, the amount of sugar (glucose) in the body is very carefully controlled. We obtain sugar from the food we eat, either from sweet things, or after the digestion of starch foods (carbohydrates), such as bread and potatoes. Under certain circumstances, however, sugar can be made in the body by breaking down body stores. This will occur when the food supply is reduced, or when more sugar is needed, such as following an injury or during an illness.

The conversion of sugar to energy requires the presence of the hormone insulin, which is produced by the pancreas. Insulin is released when the blood sugar rises after a meal, and its level falls when the blood sugar decreases (Fig. 1.4), for example during exercise. Therefore, it can be seen that insulin plays a vital role in maintaining the correct level of blood sugar, particularly by preventing the blood sugar from rising too high. When there is a shortage of insulin, or if the available insulin does not function correctly, then diabetes will result.

Fig. 1.4
Blood sugar and insulin levels rise and fall after each meal or snack.

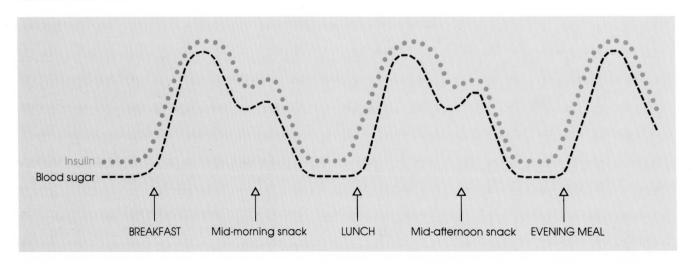

Insulin ● ● ● ●
Blood sugar – – – –

BREAKFAST   Mid-morning snack   LUNCH   Mid-afternoon snack   EVENING MEAL

The consequences of diabetes are summarized below:

1. Because the blood sugar is not converted to energy, the amount of sugar in the blood builds up and spills into the urine.
2. In an attempt to compensate for the lack of energy, the liver makes much more sugar than normal.
3. Since there is an inadequate amount of insulin to convert the sugar to energy, another energy source has to be found. The body's stores of fat and protein are therefore broken down to release more sugar into the bloodstream, and there is a consequent loss of weight.
4. In the complete absence of insulin, the breakdown of fats may be excessive and substances called ketones — the breakdown products of fatty acids — will be found in the blood and will spill into the urine.

Some ketones are acids, and if very large amounts are present, as for example in severe insulin deficiency, they cause the very serious condition of diabetic keto-acidosis or diabetic coma.

Type of diabetes

There are two main types of diabetes:

1. Non-insulin dependent diabetes — also known as Type II diabetes or maturity onset diabetes.
2. Insulin dependent diabetes — also known as Type I diabetes or juvenile diabetes.

The essential difference between these two types is that people with insulin dependent diabetes, because they produce little or no insulin, will not survive unless they are treated with insulin. This is exactly what happened to people with diabetes before insulin treatment started in 1922.

In non-insulin dependent diabetes insulin is still produced, although it may be in inadequate amounts, or it may not be working properly. These people do not need insulin in order to survive and, in most cases, can be effectively treated by diet, or by a combination of diet and tablets. Only rarely do people with non-insulin dependent diabetes require insulin in order to establish perfect control.

The causes of diabetes and who gets it

In the United Kingdom, as many as 1 to 2 per cent of the population, and perhaps one in every 500 schoolchildren, have diabetes. It can occur at any age, but it is very rare in infants and becomes much commoner in the middle and older age groups. Amongst younger people, the sexes are almost equally affected by diabetes, whereas in older age groups, diabetes is commoner in women.

Non-insulin dependent diabetes

Cause

In this type of diabetes there is some insulin in the body, but not enough to maintain good health. The cause is not known.

Who gets it?

Non-insulin dependent diabetes used to be called 'maturity onset diabetes', indicating that it occurs in the middle and older age groups, although it occasionally occurs in young people. Overweight people are particularly likely to develop this type of diabetes, as are members of certain families in whom the condition is passed from one generation to the next.

Insulin dependent diabetes

Cause

In this type of diabetes there is a complete or near complete absence of insulin, due to destruction of the insulin-producing cells of the pancreas. There is some tendency for insulin dependent diabetes to run in families, but the condition is far from being entirely inherited. The exact cause of the damage to the insulin-producing cells is not known for certain, but a combination of factors may be involved including:

- Damage to the insulin-producing cells, as a result of viral and other infections
- An abnormal reaction of the body against the insulin-producing cells.

Who gets it?

In general, younger people with diabetes (less than 40 years of age) are usually insulin dependent, but all age groups, even the very old, may be affected.

Other causes of diabetes

Diseases of the pancreas

A very few cases of diabetes are due to various diseases of the pancreas, such as inflammation of the pancreas (pancreatitis), or unusual deposits of iron. Occasionally, it occurs in rare forms of hormone imbalance.

Accidents or illnesses

Major accidents or illnesses are not thought to cause diabetes but, by causing a temporary increase in blood sugar, they may reveal pre-existing diabetes, or make worse established diabetes. If your diabetes was discovered during the course of an illness, it is highly likely that you had diabetes before the illness, even though you did not show any symptoms.

Occasionally, during very severe illnesses such as a heart attack, a serious injury, or after a major operation, the blood sugar may rise, producing a state of temporary diabetes.

Psychological stress is not believed to cause diabetes, but may certainly exacerbate it.

Drugs

Some drugs can increase the blood sugar and may reveal pre-existing diabetes. Cortisone-like (steroid) drugs commonly do this, while water tablets (diuretics), which eliminate fluid from the body, do so less commonly. There are no other commonly used drugs which have this effect.

The contraceptive pill

The oral contraceptive pill does not cause diabetes, but it may raise the blood sugar slightly in those who already have the condition.

Heredity

Hereditary factors have already been briefly mentioned. The risk that the child of a father or mother who takes insulin may develop some type of diabetes before 20 years of age is higher than normal, but is still very small, probably about 1 per cent. In the rare situation where both parents have this type of diabetes the risk is further increased, but by an uncertain amount, and in such cases professional genetic counselling may be sought.

In the more common, non-insulin dependent diabetes, the situation is somewhat different, in that the condition is predominantly inherited. Because this type of diabetes usually occurs in people who are middle-aged or older, there are relatively few women of child-bearing age with non-insulin dependent diabetes.

So, to summarize, it is possible for someone to inherit a proneness to diabetes, but not the condition itself, which will only develop as a result of the influence of some other factor. Thus, there are a large number of people who never develop diabetes, even though they have an inherited tendency to do so.

Onset of symptoms and their severity

The main symptoms of diabetes are:

- Thirst and a dry mouth
- Passing large amounts of urine
- Weight loss
- Tiredness
- Itching of the genital organs
- Blurring of vision.

Symptoms vary considerably in their severity and rate of onset.

Non-insulin dependent diabetes

The symptoms develop more gradually and are usually less severe than in insulin dependent diabetes.
Diabetic coma does not occur in this type of diabetes.

Some people fail to notice any symptoms, but after being treated they usually have more energy and feel considerably better.
Unfortunately, the presence of symptoms is no guide to the level of sugar in the blood, and it is essential that diabetes is treated, even when there are no symptoms.

During an illness, usually an infection such as a chest or urinary infection, the symptoms of non-insulin dependent diabetes may worsen. In such instances, routine treatment by diet alone may prove inadequate, and tablets or insulin may prove necessary temporarily.

Insulin dependent diabetes

The condition develops fairly quickly, usually over a few weeks, but it may take as little as a few days, or as long as several months. Without insulin treatment the condition progressively worsens, resulting in a significant weight loss, dehydration, vomiting, the onset of drowsiness, and diabetic coma.

Treatment

Diabetes is a very common disorder. **Although no 'cure' is possible, all types of diabetes can be treated and normal health restored.**

Treatment is with:

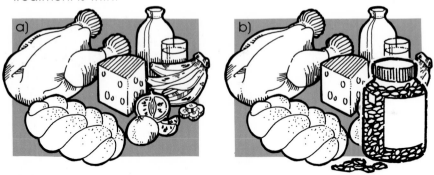

● Diet or diet and tablets — for non-insulin dependent diabetes

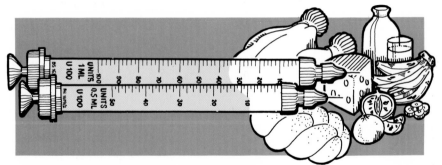

● Insulin and diet — for insulin dependent diabetes.

Treatment must be maintained throughout life. This is necessary not only to avoid symptoms and the risk of coma, but also to minimize the risks of any later complications.

All forms of treatment require some modification to daily routines, and the performance of checks to ensure that treatment is effective. However, you should be able to achieve these with only minimal disturbance to your daily life.

From Chapter 2 onwards, this Handbook explains in detail what has gone wrong in your type of diabetes and describes how, with correct treatment, you should be able to maintain effective control.

Non-insulin dependent diabetes

To understand the causes of non-insulin dependent diabetes, and to appreciate how you can manage your treatment, it is necessary to know some basic facts about the food you eat, how it is broken down in the body, how it is used and what may have gone wrong to cause your diabetes.

Some basic facts about nutrition

Our food is made up of three basic types — carbohydrates, fats and proteins, all of which are essential for a balanced diet (Fig. 2.1). As Fig. 2.2 shows, these three types of food are broken down by digestive processes in the intestinal tract and absorbed into the blood stream. For example, carbohydrates — the starchy foods, such as bread and potatoes — are broken down and converted to simple sugars, such as glucose, by the digestive juices of the mouth, stomach and intestines. The breakdown products of digestion are then absorbed into the blood stream and carried to the individual body cells. Fig. 2.2 shows that sugars and fatty acids provide energy, while amino acids, often referred to as the body's 'building blocks', are used to build cells and tissues and in excess are converted to glucose.

Fig. 2.1
Carbohydrates, fats and proteins are essential for a balanced diet.

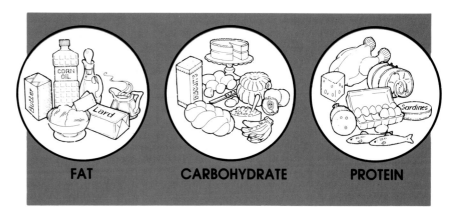

FAT   CARBOHYDRATE   PROTEIN

The whole process of food breakdown and usage, and the excretion of waste products, is termed metabolism. Metabolism is extremely complex, and in the healthy individual is very finely balanced, so that the body functions smoothly. Any imbalance in the metabolism of one type of food produces an effect on the metabolism of other types of food. For example, if the body is unable to convert sugar to energy, then the metabolism of fat and protein will be affected. In fact, this is exactly what happens in diabetes.

What has gone wrong?

In Chapter 1 the role of sugar control in the development of diabetes was briefly considered, and it is now appropriate to examine the significance of sugar metabolism in more detail. A basic knowledge of sugar metabolism is the key to understanding diabetes, so it is worthwhile carefully reading and re-reading the next few pages until the process is clear in your mind.

Where does blood sugar come from?

In the healthy individual, the level of blood sugar is kept within close limits, but will obviously be at its lowest several hours after a meal, and at its highest just after a meal. Under normal circumstances, the main source of blood sugar is the food we eat:

- **Sweet things** e.g. sugar added to cereals, drinks, sweets, jams, etc.

- **Starch foods** e.g. bread, potatoes, cereals, flour, etc.

- **Other foods** e.g. protein, may be converted to glucose.

Fig. 2.2 shows that sugar is absorbed into the blood supply and is transported to the individual body cells, where it is used for the production of energy. Excess sugar is converted to fat (triglyceride) and stored in the fat stores of the body, or it is converted to starch (glycogen), which is stored in the liver, for use as an energy supply in time of need. Eating too much overall increases the blood sugar and the weight.

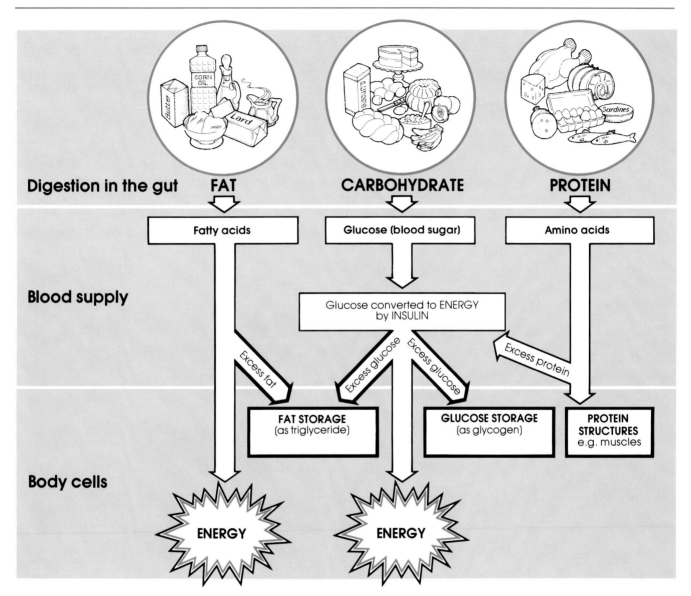

Fig. 2.2
Normal metabolism.

In the presence of insulin, glucose can be converted to energy.

The role of insulin

The key to the conversion of sugar to energy, or its storage as starch and fat, is insulin. Insulin, however, not only enables sugar to be converted to energy but also helps to increase the amount of stored energy, by preventing excessive breakdown of fat.

Insulin is produced by the pancreas, a gland situated at the back of the abdomen, and having the structure shown in Fig. 2.3. The pancreas is able to sense the level of blood sugar, and when this rises it will push more insulin into the circulation. Thus, the level of insulin is highest just after a meal and lowest when fasting or during exercise (Fig. 2.4). In your type of diabetes, although you are producing insulin, the supply is insufficient to cope with demand

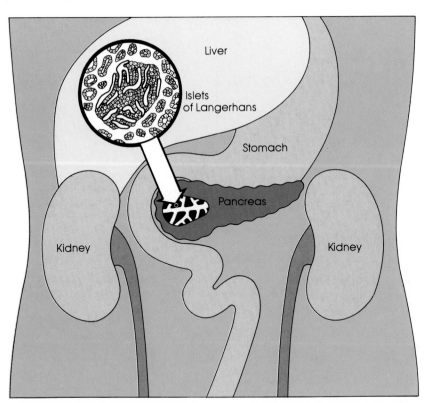

Fig. 2.3
The pancreas.
The pancreas is a large gland positioned behind the stomach. The inset shows the detailed structure of the insulin-producing cells, the islets of Langerhans.

Fig. 2.4
Insulin released from the pancreas makes the blood sugar level fall.

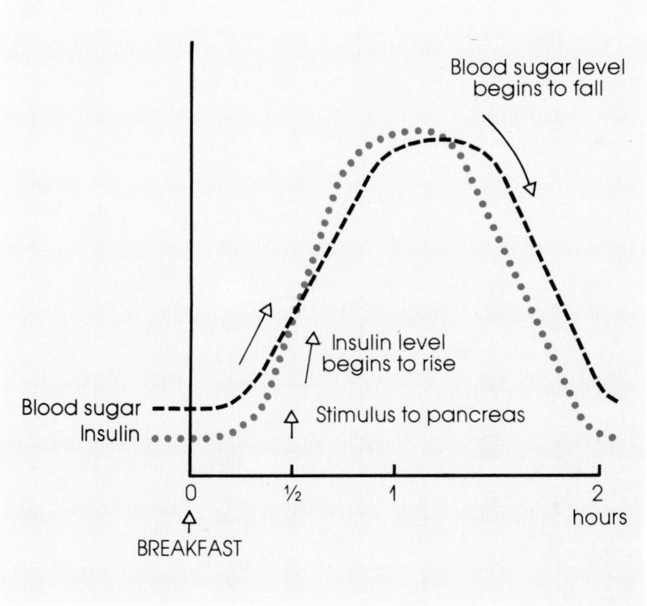

Fig. 2.5
In diabetes, insufficient insulin results in an excessively high blood sugar.

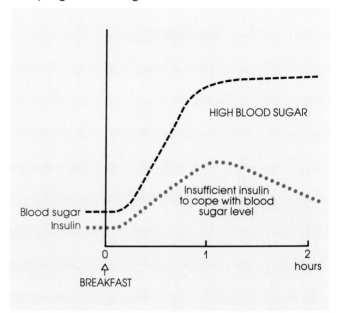

and this leads to a partial failure in the conversion of blood sugar to energy (Fig. 2.5). As you eat, therefore, the sugar level in the blood increases to a higher than normal level (hyperglycaemia). This is the hallmark of diabetes — an excessively high blood sugar.

Who gets diabetes and why?

There may be two contributory factors to the development of your diabetes:

1. The pancreas may produce enough insulin, but it does not work effectively.

2. The pancreas may be unable to produce enough insulin to maintain the blood sugar within the normal range.

Non-insulin dependent diabetes occurs in various groups of individuals:

- It occurs most commonly in people who are overweight. The reason for this is that fat tissue interferes with the action of insulin, so that overweight people need considerably more insulin than normal individuals. If, in addition, an overweight person has a less than normal production of insulin, because of a defect in the pancreas, then clearly the supply of insulin will be insufficient to prevent the development of diabetes. Also, because some overweight people tend to over-eat, the supply of sugar may be too high to be processed by the available insulin. In most cases, this type of diabetes can be readily controlled by simply eating less and losing weight, thereby allowing the insulin to work more effectively.

- This type of diabetes also occurs in people who are not over-weight but who produce inadequate amounts of insulin.

- Some people are predisposed to diabetes by a tendency to be unable to produce enough insulin. This tendency may only become obvious at times when more sugar than normal is required, such as during an illness or after injury. It is important to stress that injury or illness are not believed to cause the diabetes, but rather they make it more obvious.

- In a few families, there is a strong hereditary element, and diabetes may be passed from generation to generation.

- It appears to be more common in some parts of the world, such as South America or Malta, than others, for example, Alaska.

Symptoms of high blood sugar

Sugar in the urine

As the blood sugar rises above normal, there comes a point when it begins to spill over into the urine (glycosuria).

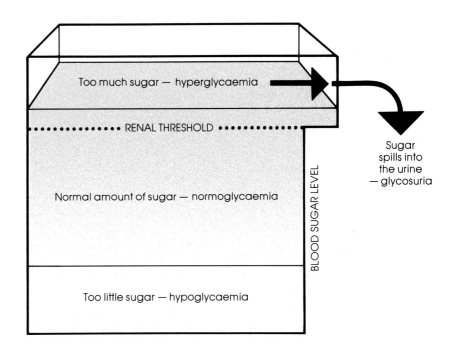

Fig. 2.6
Blood sugar levels.
When the blood sugar reaches a certain level it spills over into the urine.
This level is called the renal threshold.

Usually, no sugar appears in the urine, unless the kidneys are malfunctioning. In a person with diabetes, however, the excess sugar is allowed to pass into the urine (Fig. 2.6), and this gives rise to three of the commonest symptoms of diabetes:

● **Passing large quantities of urine**
In order to get rid of the excess sugar, more water is excreted by the kidneys, and this results in the frequent passing of large volumes of urine. It may cause bed-wetting in some children, and incontinence in the elderly.

Thirst

Because more water is leaving the body, the mouth becomes dry and thirst develops. The sensation may be so intense and disagreeable that sometimes even talking and swallowing become difficult. Soft drinks which contain a lot of sugar should be avoided, because they actually increase the blood sugar, resulting in an even greater thirst.

Genital soreness

When a large quantity of sugar is passed in the urine, it tends to cause irritation around the genital area, and thrush may develop. It frequently causes itching of the vulva in women and, less frequently, itching of the penis in men. However, once diabetes is controlled and sugar disappears from the urine, these problems usually disappear.

Breakdown of body energy stores

Because a shortage of insulin means that the blood sugar cannot be converted into energy, energy must be provided from elsewhere. Consequently, there is a breakdown of fat and protein which results in:

Weight loss

Diabetes is one of the commonest causes of weight loss. This occurs in most people with diabetes at the onset of the disorder. It ranges from a few pounds to 2 or 3 stone. Appetite is commonly unaffected and may even be increased, but not everyone loses weight, so do not ignore other symptoms.

Tiredness and weakness

Tiredness, often accompanied by a sensation of weakness, is very common in uncontrolled diabetes. Some people are more than usually prone to fall asleep at odd times, while others just feel they are growing old before their time. This symptom can be readily reversed by treatment. Many feel 'rejuvenated' after treatment, even when they had previously been unaware of any abnormalities.

Other effects of high blood sugar

These include:

- **Blurring of vision**

  The high level of sugar in the body causes the lens of the eye to change slightly in shape. Some people with diabetes become short-sighted when they first develop the disorder, but the reverse sometimes occurs, making reading difficult. These changes may only be noticed in the early stages of the treatment, and normally the ability to focus is completely restored in two or three weeks. It is wise, however, not to have your eyes tested for at least two months after proper stabilization of the diabetes.

- **Excessive loss of fluid/diabetic coma**

  It is important to stress that in your type of diabetes, the so-called 'diabetic coma', which results from an extremely high blood sugar level, does not occur. Very rarely, if a vomiting illness, such as gastroenteritis, coincides with the development of your diabetes, then the blood sugar level may become unusually high. This can cause a significant increase in fluid loss, which may require hospital treatment. If you are eating normally, however, excessive fluid loss should not occur.

Symptomless diabetes

Most people with diabetes are aware of symptoms when the blood sugar is very high, but others may be quite unaware of their condition. For instance, diabetes is often detected at a routine medical examination for insurance or employment purposes, or during an investigation of some quite unrelated illness.

Long-term effects of high blood sugar

If the blood sugar remains high for a period of years — even if it is not causing symptoms — it may cause damage. Particularly common are: damage to the small blood vessels in the feet; damage to the small nerves, creating a tingling sensation in the feet; or the development of a cataract. Early, effective treatment of diabetes should prevent these from developing. Where they have already developed, the sooner they are detected, the more effective will be their treatment.

Complications of diabetes are considered in more detail in Chapter 5, page 63.

Treatment

Aims of treatment

There are two main aims of treatment:

1. Eliminate symptoms
The high blood sugar level is largely responsible for the symptoms of diabetes. Therefore, the first aim of treatment is to reverse any symptoms you might have, by returning the blood sugar level to normal. Once treatment has started, your feeling of well-being will be restored, any tendency to develop infections will be minimized, and, as long as treatment is continued, there should be no recurrence of symptoms.

2. Prevent late complications
If a high blood sugar is maintained over many years, then the eyes, kidneys and small nerves to the feet may be damaged. Clearly, there is every reason for returning your blood sugar level to normal and, by keeping to your treatment, reducing the risk of these complications.

IT IS IMPORTANT THAT YOU CONTINUE WITH YOUR TREATMENT, EVEN WHEN THE SYMPTOMS HAVE GONE, AND THAT YOU UNDERGO REGULAR CHECKS TO ENSURE THAT YOUR CONTROL IS BEING MAINTAINED.

The steps you need to take

Diet

● **Reduce your weight**

Most people with non-insulin dependent diabetes are overweight, and therefore the most important measure needed to control blood sugar levels is to reduce weight by dieting, and then to maintain it at the desired level. Your aim should be to reach a point where the insulin you produce is able to maintain your blood sugar at a normal level.

- **Control your sugar intake**

  This means avoiding or reducing the amount of those foods in the diet which lead to a rise in blood sugar, particularly sweets and refined sugars.

- **Reduce your fat intake**

  Cut back on fats and fatty foods if you are overweight.

- **Balance your diet**

  It is important that you ensure that the food you eat provides the right balance, so that you not only avoid those items which increase the blood sugar, but also an excess of other foodstuffs which might cause damage in other ways.

All of these essential adjustments to your diet can be achieved fairly easily, and you can continue to eat interesting and pleasant food.

Exercise

If you are able, it is important that you should take regular exercise. This will not only help to keep your blood sugar low but, if you are overweight, will also help you reduce your weight.

Other treatment measures

- **Tablets**

  If the above measures prove inadequate, you may be advised to take some special tablets to increase the efficiency of your diet.

- **Insulin injections**

  Insulin injections are not required, except occasionally when all the above measures have proved unsuccessful.

DIET

Let us now consider the importance of diet in more detail. To help you find a balanced diet which will enable you to control your diabetes, it is necessary to understand the basic facts about food and how it is broken down and used by the body.

The basic components of food

As outlined in Chapter 2, page 11, our food is made up of three basic types, namely carbohydrates, proteins and fats, all of which are essential for a balanced diet. Many foods contain mixtures of one or more types. For example, milk is made up of carbohydrate, protein and fat, eggs contain fat and protein, and pastry is mainly fat and carbohydrate. In general, vegetables and fruit contain little or no fat, while cheese, margarine and meat contain no carbohydrate.

Carbohydrate

Carbohydrate is found in:

- Sweet foods, such as sugar, jams and sweetened manufactured foods (Fig. 3.1)
- Starch foods, such as potatoes, cereal and pastry (Fig. 3.2)
- Some fruit and vegetables (Fig. 3.2).

Fig. 3.1
Carbohydrates: some typical foods containing large amounts of sugar.

Fig. 3.2
Carbohydrates: some typical
starch-containing foods.

Protein

Protein is provided in such foods as meat, eggs, fish (Fig. 3.3), dairy products and some vegetables. Some protein in the diet is essential, because it provides the building materials for the cells and tissues of the body.

Fig. 3.3
Common foods containing mainly
protein.

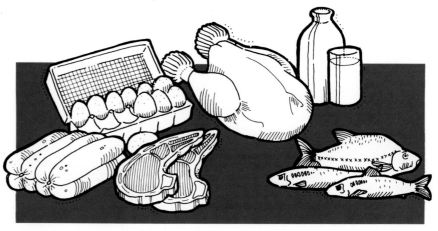

Fat

As well as obvious sources of fat (Fig. 3.4), such as butter, margarine, oil, lard and dripping, most meats, dairy products and eggs contain fat. Because even small amounts of fat contain a large number of calories, only small quantities are absolutely necessary for the maintenance of good health.

Fig. 3.4
Common foods containing a lot of fat.

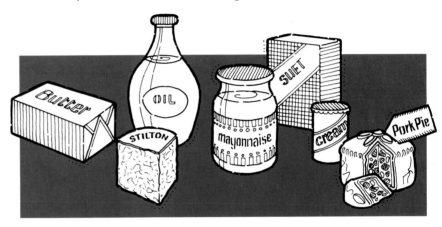

Other important components of the diet

These include:

Minerals and vitamins

With the right balance of carbohydrate, protein and fat, minerals and vitamins will be automatically included and supplements will not be necessary.

Fibre

This provides much of the bulk in most vegetables and some fruit, and is present in large quantities in unrefined cereal. Unfortunately, much of the fibre may be removed during modern food processing, a good example being the making of white flour and the milling of rice. Fibre is particularly valuable in diabetes, as it moderates the absorption of food.

Which foods should you eat?

The foods you eat should be determined by your weight. The diet for people with diabetes who are overweight is somewhat different from that for those with diabetes who are of normal weight. But, whatever your weight, you should avoid all very sweet foods and drinks, which cause a rapid rise in blood sugar.

If you are overweight, you should read the next section (light blue pages); if, however, your weight is normal, you should turn to the section beginning on page 35.

DIET IF YOU ARE OVERWEIGHT

Principles

The adjustments to your diet are based on the following two principles:

1. Avoid very sweet foods and drinks (Table 1), thereby minimizing the amount of sugar which has to be disposed of by your reduced insulin supply.

TABLE 1 Foods to be avoided

The foods listed below are high in sugar and have virtually no nutritional value:

Marmalade*/jam*/honey*/mincemeat/lemon curd
Golden syrup/black treacle
Sugar/glucose/glucose tablets
Fizzy and mixer drinks*, cordials* and squashes*, unless marked 'no sugar'/'low calorie'.
Bottled sauces and chutneys (in large amounts)
Buns/pastries/sweet biscuits
Sweets and chocolates
Fruit tinned in syrup*
*Low-sugar alternatives are available.

---

2. <u>Lose weight by reducing your intake of all those foods which provide energy in excess of your requirements,</u> so that your body will be forced to burn off its own fat. In other words, you will have to eat less food — particularly fats and sugary carbohydrate. Your dietitian or doctor will calculate how much food you will require to provide a balanced diet, supply sufficient energy, and allow you to lose weight. Very often a calorie allowance will be suggested.

Once you have reached your desired weight, your diet will be altered to that suitable for a person of normal weight. <u>However, it is important that your weight remains constant,</u> so make regular checks and if your weight increases, cut back as previously advised.

Some basic facts

Losing weight is never easy, particularly at first, but the more you know about foods and diet, the better you will be able to cope.

● Different people need different amounts of food. It may seem unfair that, even though you are already eating less than a slim person, you are still overweight. However, the fact remains that, in order to lose weight, you will need to eat less food than your body needs, thereby causing you to burn up your own excess fat.

A good guide to start with is to avoid fatty and sugary foods as much as possible, and to have smaller quantities of food at each meal.

● It takes time to become overweight, so you should not expect to lose weight very quickly. A loss of one or two pounds (one kilogram) a week is perfectly adequate. At first, you may lose weight faster, perhaps as much as three quarters of a stone (5-6 kilograms) in the first month, but subsequently your weight loss will probably slow down. Do not become discouraged — continue with the diet until it shows the final results that you are aiming for.

● Many people believe that some foods are slimming and others fattening. This is not strictly true, since all foods, if taken in the wrong amounts, can cause problems. Therefore, it is important to learn which foods will help you to lose weight, how much of each you can eat at any one time, and also the best way of cooking each type of food.

- A restriction of fluid intake is sometimes advised, because excess fluid is often blamed for weight gain. This is quite unnecessary, however, and a normal intake of fluid is recommended, taking care to avoid sweetened or malted drinks.

Some dietary guidelines

To help you decide what to eat in order to ensure balanced, nutritious meals, but at the same time control your calorie intake, we have divided the various foods into four main groups:

1. Carbohydrate starch foods

2. Dairy products

3. Protein and fat foods

4. Fruit and vegetables.

Carbohydrates

- This group includes flour, bread, pasta, rice, potatoes and breakfast cereals, as well as sweet foods which should, of course, be avoided (Fig. 3.5).

- This is one of the most important groups in your weight-reducing diet, and at least three small helpings from this group should be taken every day. A complete list is given in Appendix 2, page 99.

- You cannot and must not try to control your diabetes by avoiding starch foods altogether, but some limitation will be necessary.

- Recent evidence has indicated that the best choice from this group would be the wholegrain cereals, such as those found in wholemeal bread, wholemeal flour, and the wholewheat breakfast cereals, for example, Shredded Wheat, Puffed Wheat, Bran Flakes, and All Bran. It is thought that the presence of fibre in these foods reduces the rate of release of sugar into the blood after digestion, and this is much better for controlling diabetes. Those carbohydrates rich in fibre are listed in Appendix 2, page 99.

Fig. 3.5
Some common carbohydrate foods

- It is important to remember that potatoes do not deserve their label as 'fattening', as an average boiled or jacket potato contains a similar amount of calories to a very small portion of meat or fish. You should, however, avoid potatoes which have had fat added to them, e.g. chipped and roast potatoes.
- You must avoid sweet and sugar foods, such as cakes, soft drinks, jams etc. (see Table 1).
- Diabetic products should also be avoided, as they are high in calories. Avoid products with the statement 'Not suitable for over-weight diabetics' on them.
- Packet and bottled sauces may be high in sugar and calories and should be avoided.

Dairy products

- This important group, which includes milk, cheese and yoghurt (Fig. 3.6), can contribute far too many calories to your daily diet and should be carefully controlled.

- Milk is a useful food to include every day, but half a pint is sufficient. If larger quantities are needed, skimmed or semi-skimmed milk can be used.

- Cheese is high in calories and should only be taken as the main portion of a meal, in place of meat, fish or poultry. The amount to have at any one time is about the size of a small matchbox. If preferred, a more generous helping of cottage cheese or reduced-fat soft cheese can be taken instead.

- Yoghurt is a popular dairy product and can be included in a weight-reducing diet, but it is better to buy plain, unsweetened or reduced-calorie yoghurt and add a small helping of fruit, rather than to use sweetened fruit yoghurt which is much higher in calories and often less filling.

- Other milk products, such as evaporated milk, can be taken in small quantities, but sweetened dairy products, for instance condensed milk, must be avoided.

Fig. 3.6
Dairy products should be eaten with caution.

Protein foods

- This group includes meat, fish, poultry and eggs, all of which contain a large number of calories (see Appendix 2). It is usually sufficient to have one or two small helpings from this group each day (Fig. 3.7).

- Ensure that all fat is trimmed from the meat, and that fat or oil is skimmed from the cooked dishes whenever possible.

- Fish tends to be low in fat, and even the oilier fish, such as mackerel, when grilled or baked as opposed to fried, is suitable.

- Some meat products, such as sausages, paté and tinned meats contain more fat than most other meats, and therefore should not be eaten more frequently than once or twice a week.

- It is important to remember that margarine, butter, oil and lard all contain large amounts of calories and should be used very sparingly. Half a pound of butter or margarine should last at least two to three weeks. Many people find that the low-fat spreads such as Outline, Gold, Slimspread etc. are useful alternatives, but even so the amounts to be taken in any one day should still be carefully controlled.

Fig. 3.7
Protein foods.

Fruit and vegetables

● This group (Fig. 3.8) forms a particularly valuable dietary constituent, because most fruit and vegetables are low calorie foods, which also have the advantage of adding bulk to the diet.

● A selection of fruit and vegetables should be included in the daily diet.

Fig. 3.8
Fruit and vegetables are essential
for a healthy diet.

Cooking

The method of cooking is very important. Ideal cooking methods are braising, stewing, dry roasting, grilling, baking in foil, poaching and scrambling.

Frying and roasting should be avoided — for example, fried or roast potatoes are much more fattening than boiled or baked potatoes. A useful maxim is: <u>avoid the frying pan — grill instead.</u>

Useful hints when starting your diet

The first few weeks of your diet will be the most difficult to cope with. Not only will you have to plan your eating pattern carefully, but you will have to resist the temptation to eat those foods which could prove harmful. Here are some hints to help you through this difficult initial period of your diet:

● **Never miss meals**

This only makes you more hungry and therefore more likely to eat extra later on. When you diet, it is important to continue the diet long enough to show weight loss. If you diet too strictly and miss meals, you might be discouraged and give up after only a week. This would achieve nothing.

● **Reduce your portions of food**

Get used to smaller portions and fill up on the foods which you can safely eat in larger quantities, such as vegetables and salad.

● **Do not buy special slimming products**

These are unnecessary and in many cases are very expensive. It is better to learn which every-day foods you can eat.

● **Plan your diet**

Discuss your diet with the person who is cooking for you and ask them to help you by planning meals accordingly. If you are in charge of the cooking, ensure you cook the right amount of food, so there are no leftovers available for second helpings.

● **Get used to eating more slowly**

The slower you eat, the fuller you are likely to feel and the less likely you are to nibble snacks afterwards.

● **Avoid impulsive eating**

A dangerous time is when you are out shopping. Always try to have something to eat before you go out, then you will be less tempted by the rows of food you should avoid!

● Snack on the right sort of food

If you get hungry, eat an extra slice of bread or an extra piece of fruit, rather than something more concentrated, such as cake, sweets or cheese.

If you do break your diet, just once, it is not the end of the world, and you can always start again at the next meal.

● Get your family to co-operate

You are dieting to improve your health. This can also be of value to your family, so enlist their assistance in helping you with your diet. If you have the family's co-operation, you can all eat the same meals. For instance, whereas you might have served steak and kidney pudding, you can offer steak and kidney instead.

● Don't dream about food!

When you are dieting, it is easy to become obsessed by food. Try to keep your mind on other things by being busy.

● Avoid diabetic foods

Most are high in calories (see page 52).

● Be careful which sugar substitutes you use

Many are suitable, but some should be avoided (see page 52).

● Take care with alcohol

Alcohol is high in calories (see page 53).

● When eating out, select your food carefully

Avoid sweet and fatty foods (see page 51).

Summary

Dieting is never easy, but the time and effort required will, in due course, be amply rewarded. By tackling your weight problem now, you will not only help to control your diabetes, but will also probably make a significant improvement in your general health and feeling of well-being.

Now is also the time to learn which foods you should and should not eat, and the most suitable method of cooking them.

DIET IF YOUR WEIGHT IS NORMAL

Principles

Your food can be divided into three groups:

> Food which should be avoided completely, except in the case of emergencies like hypo's or on special occasions, e.g. food containing large amounts of sugar.

> Food which can be eaten with some care and regulated to a certain extent, e.g. refined starch carbohydrate (low in fibre) and full-fat milk and milk products, and some fats.

> Food which can be eaten regularly as part of the diet.

To help you identify the group to which a particular food belongs, a colour coding system is used throughout this section. Thus, foods to be avoided are keyed with red, yellow indicates foods to be eaten with caution or regulated, and green identifies foods which may be eaten regularly.

The diet you follow should enable you to maintain your weight without causing you to feel hungry. Such a diet will have to be worked out with you, in the first instance, by your doctor or dietitian, who will suggest a specific carbohydrate allowance, but some general guidelines are given below.

Foods to be avoided

Avoid all very sweet foods and drinks, which cause a rapid rise in blood sugar except in the case of hypo's.

By cutting out sweet foods you are minimizing the amount of sugar which has to be disposed of by your reduced insulin supply. A detailed list of these is given in Table 2 opposite.

Fig. 3.9
A range of common foods which, because of their high sugar content, should be avoided.

a. Sweets and chocolates have a very high sugar content, especially fruit drops and pastilles.

b. These foods rapidly affect the blood sugar. Honey is often mistakenly believed to be suitable for those with diabetes.

c. Asian and West Indian sweetmeats, which are offered as part of hospitality and at festivals, should be eaten as 'small tastes' only.

d. Sweet biscuits and cakes should be substituted with high-fibre, low-sugar alternatives.

e. Instant desserts and sweetened cereals should be replaced with unsweetened alternatives.

f. These highly sweetened drinks should be avoided.

TABLE 2 Foods to be avoided

The foods listed below are high in sugar and have virtually no nutritional value:

Marmalade */jam */honey *

Mincemeat/lemon curd

Golden syrup

Black treacle

Sugar

Glucose

Glucose tablets

Fizzy and mixer drinks *, cordials * and squashes *, unless marked 'no sugar'/'low calorie'.

Minerals *

Coca-Cola *

Lemonade *

Tonic *, ginger ale *, bitter lemon * etc.

Bottled sauces and chutneys (in large amounts)

Buns

Pastries

Sweet biscuits

Sweets and chocolates

Fruit tinned in syrup *

*Low-sugar alternatives are available.

For further information refer to 'Countdown', published by the British Diabetic Association.

Fig. 3.10
Some examples of foods containing
10g (1 'exchange') of carbohydrate.

Foods to be eaten with care and in regulated amounts

Carbohydrates

How much carbohydrate?

The first point to remember is that your diet must contain enough carbohydrate to ensure a reasonable level of blood sugar, in order to provide the fuel your body needs. You **CANNOT** cut out all foods providing sugar. This would merely induce your body to make more sugar from its reserves, thereby causing you to lose weight and become unwell. Starvation is no treatment for any type of diabetes.

The total amount of carbohydrate you need will be determined for you. Usually almost half your total energy (calorie) requirement is supplied by carbohydrates. This will be subdivided so that you take most of it at main meals and smaller amounts at snack times. To help you control your carbohydrate intake, and still enjoy a varied and interesting diet, a system of 'exchanges' (also called 'portions', 'rations', or 'lines') is used. If you look at Table 3, page 40, carbohydrates have been listed in simple household measures, i.e. tablespoons, cups, slices etc, so that each measure of whichever type of food you prefer contains 10 g of carbohydrate, called a 'portion' or an 'exchange'. All of these are equivalent (Fig. 3.10). Thus, one Weetabix is equivalent to one thin slice of bread, one egg-sized potato or two tablespoons of flour. A more detailed list is given in Appendix 2, page 99.

If it has been decided that you need five portions for each main meal, you can then simply select those you prefer, e.g. two portions of bread, two of cereal and one of fruit, or any other mixture. Your snacks can be similarly varied. In these calculations you should not forget additions, such as milk with cereal.

It is not necessary to weigh food. With the help of lists and advice from your dietitian, you should not find difficulty in basing your quantities on household measures.

TABLE 3 Carbohydrate exchanges [†]

Foods in this list contain carbohydrate (starch) in substantial amounts.

These foods are listed in exchanges, which are equal in carbohydrate value, so you may 'exchange' any of these for another on your daily menu.

Each exchange = 10g of carbohydrate

High-fibre foods are marked: *good fibre content
                                          **very good fibre content

<u>Spoon measures are standard kitchen spoons.</u>

Bread and biscuits
*1 small slice of wholemeal bread [††]
*½ large thick slice of bread [††]
*1 small roll [††]
2 crispbreads
*1 digestive or wholemeal biscuit
2 cream crackers or water biscuits
2 plain or semi-sweet biscuits

Cereals
**2 level tablespoons wholemeal flour
1½ level tablespoons white flour
**3 level tablespoons uncooked porridge
4 tablespoons wholemeal breakfast cereal, e.g. **Branflakes
**12 Shreddies
**1 Weetabix or ⅔ Shredded Wheat
2 tablespoons cooked pasta, e.g. macaroni
2 level tablespoons cooked rice
1 level tablespoon custard powder
2 level teaspoons sago/tapioca/semolina
Choose wholemeal bread, wholewheat pasta or brown rice where possible, as they are rich in fibre.

Vegetables

**4 level tablespoons baked beans
**2 level tablespoons lentils (before cooking)
**4 level tablespoons tinned or well cooked 'dried' beans
2 small beetroot
1 small parsnip
1 egg-sized potato (boiled, roast)
1 scoop mashed potato
*1 small jacket potato
**½ medium corn-on-the-cob
**5 tablespoons sweetcorn

Fruit

1 apple, 1 orange, 1 pear, 1 peach, 1 small banana, 10 grapes, 12 cherries, 2 dessert plums, **2 large prunes, 1 slice pineapple, 15 strawberries, 2 tangerines
*2 level tablespoons currants, raisins or sultanas
1 small bowl stewed fruit
1 small glass (4 fluid oz) fruit juice, (e.g. apple, grapefruit, orange, pineapple)
4-6 chestnuts

Milk

1 cup (⅓ pint) whole or skimmed milk
1 carton (small) plain yoghurt or ½ carton fruit yoghurt
6 tablespoons (3 fluid oz) evaporated milk

Miscellaneous

Use these only occasionally to make up your exchanges, as they contain a lot of fat, a lot of sugar, or are low in fibre.

1 cup of soup (tinned or packet)	2 sausages
2 level teaspoons Horlicks, Ovaltine	4 large chips
2 bun-size batter puddings	
1 small brickette (or scoop) ice cream	

† More detailed lists are available in Appendix 2, page 99.
†† Sliced bread varies according to the brand; the carbohydrate content will be found on the packaging. For further details of the carbohydrate content of these and other manufactured foods, you should refer to 'Countdown', published by the British Diabetic Association.

Fig. 3.11
The best choice of carbohydrate foods.

a. **Fibre-containing foods**

b. **Fruit and vegetables** (many of these contain fibre)

c. **Pasta and wholegrain rice**

The best choice of carbohydrates

- **Fibre** reduces the rate of release of sugar into the blood after digestion, and this, of course, is much better for diabetic control. Carbohydrates rich in fibre include the wholegrain cereals, such as those found in wholemeal bread, wholemeal flour, and whole wheat breakfast cereals, for example Shredded Wheat, Puffed Wheat, Bran Flakes and All Bran (Fig. 3.11).

  You should select from Table 3 (see also Appendix 2) those carbohydrates with a high fibre content. These should provide up to two thirds of your total carbohydrate requirements.

- **Fruit and vegetables** should always be included in the daily diet. Those that contain carbohydrate should be included in your total daily intake, as indicated in Table 3, some can be eaten in unlimited quantities (see page 47) and many are high in fibre.

Dairy Products

- **Milk** (Fig. 3.12) is a useful food to include every day, but does contain sugar (see Table 3) and must be considered as an exchange or portion.

Fig. 3.12
Dairy products should be eaten in regulated amounts.

- **Yoghurt** is a popular dairy product, but it is better to buy a reduced-sugar yoghurt, or a plain, unsweetened yoghurt and add a small helping of fruit, rather than normal sweetened fruit yoghurt which contains a lot of sugar.
- **Other milk products,** such as evaporated milk, can be taken in small quantities, but sweetened dairy products, for instance condensed milk, must be avoided.

Be extra careful with these foods

- **Fats** (Fig. 3.13a and b) should be eaten with some restraint. They are a concentrated form of calories, which easily lead to overweight, and in excess may cause other health problems.
- **Meat products** (Fig. 3.13a) which are particularly high in fat, such as sausages and meat pies, should be eaten in limited amounts. Also, you should remove the fat from the meat.
- **Cheese, cream, butter and margarine** should be limited. Do not nibble fatty foods.
  Spread butter and other spreads sparingly.
  Try replacing milk with skimmed or semi-skimmed milk.

If you feel hungry and you are not overweight, it is likely that you need more carbohydrate. It is not wise to base every meal on a large portion of meat, fish or cheese. If you are in doubt about your allowance, ask the advice of your doctor or dietitian.

Ideal cooking methods are braising, stewing, dry roasting, grilling, baking in foil, poaching or scrambling. A useful maxim is: avoid the frying pan — grill instead.

Fig. 3.13
Extra care is required when eating these foods.

a. Many popular foods contain a high level of 'hidden' fat, particularly meat products, pastry and fried food such as fish and chips.

b. Other foods with a high 'hidden' fat content, include natural foods, such as nuts and seeds, and processed foods, such as crisps.

c. All of these 'visible' fats should be limited. Full-fat milk, as used in some yoghurts, and evaporated milk are best reduced.

Foods which can be eaten regularly

Fruits and vegetables

Some fruits and most vegetables contain negligible amounts of carbohydrate, are low in calories, and can be eaten in generous quantities. Examples are listed in Table 4, opposite.

Proteins — lean meat, poultry, fish and eggs

- To have pleasant and nutritional meals, the balance of energy or calories is provided by protein (and fat). As Westerners, we eat considerably more protein than we really need.
- Providing you take care to avoid a very fat diet, lean meat, poultry, fish and eggs (Fig. 3.14a) can be eaten as normal.

Beverages

Drinks listed in Table 4, do not contain sugar. Soft drinks, listed in Table 2, should be avoided, as they contain a lot of sugar. It should be remembered that drinks taken with milk, such as tea and cocoa, contain both calories and carbohydrate.

Fig. 3.14
Foods which can be eaten regularly.

a. **Protein-containing foods** — care should be taken to limit the intake of fat.

b. **Beverages** — sugar-free mixer drinks may be drunk freely.

TABLE 4 Foods which can be eaten freely

Vegetables

Cauliflower	Marrow	Tomatoes
Runner beans	Mushrooms	Peppers
Carrots	Celery	Swede
Peas	Onions	Turnip
All green leafy vegetables		
Frozen and fresh peas		
Salad vegetables		

Fruit

Cranberries	Lemons	Rhubarb
Gooseberries	Loganberries	Redcurrants
½ Grapefruit		

Beverages

Tea	Bovril	Tomato juice
Coffee	Marmite	Lemon juice
Oxo	Soda water	Clear soups
Sugar-free squashes and 'mixers'		

Seasonings

Pepper	Pickles	Spices
Mustard	Herbs	Stock cubes
Vinegar	Essences and food colourings	

Sweetening agents

Only tablet and liquid saccharine sweetener, aspartame and acesulfame-K.

Your family's diet

Although the type of diet outlined above is designed for the specific needs of a person with diabetes, it is a particularly healthy diet in so far as it is based on a minimal sugar and fat intake, and an increase in the consumption of fruit, vegetables and fibre-containing foods. Consequently, it is recommended that the whole family should be offered the benefits of meals based on this type of diet.

Fig. 3.15
Food for people with diabetes can be enjoyed by the whole family. Such food is not only healthier, but can be just as tasty as more conventional dishes.

a. Frankfurter pizza, Mixed grill flan and Tuna flan.

b. Cottage cheese quiche and Vegetable curry.

Eating out

As your knowledge about your diet increases, you will gain more confidence about eating out, and will be able to select from the menus those foods which are most appropriate. For those of normal weight, eating out need not be restricted.

Fig. 3.16
Eating out.
With a little extra care you can eat out and still follow your diet.

If you are at all concerned about the suitability of certain foods in a restaurant, do not be afraid to ask.

Wherever possible:

- Select generous portions of vegetables

- Cut down on fats and sugar

- Choose baked, grilled or boiled food, as opposed to fried or roasted.

However, an occasional indiscretion, although it may lead to a temporary rise in blood sugar, will not do any long-term harm.

Of course, eating with friends or relatives should pose no problems. If you let them know the foods you would prefer not to eat, any embarrassment will be readily avoided.

If you need help

If you should have any problems with your diet, do not be afraid to ask for help from your doctor or dietitian. Very good guidance can be obtained from the many diabetic cookery books and from the extensive lists of foods now available, such as 'Countdown', published by the British Diabetic Association.

Summary

Your food can be divided into three groups:

> **Food which should be avoided completely, except for hypo's or special occasions, e.g. food containing large amounts of sugar.**

> **Food which can be eaten with some care and regulated to a certain extent, e.g. refined starch carbohydrate (low in fibre) and full-fat milk and milk products, and some fats.**

> **Food which can be eaten regularly as part of your diet, providing your weight does not become excessive.**

Planning your diet consists of the following steps:

- Determining the total number of carbohydrate portions per day
- Deciding when to have the portions
- Selecting the type of food suited to your taste
- Balancing meals and snacks with foods freely allowed, avoiding those containing sugar.

'Diabetic' foods

These foods are usually sweet, as cane sugar has been substituted with other sweeteners. They are best avoided, not only because they are very expensive, but because they are very often high in calories, and therefore fattening. Some specialist products, however, may add variety to the diet. These include the wide range of sugar-free drinks, fruits tinned in natural juices, reduced-sugar preserves, and sugar-free sweets and chewing gum (Fig. 3.17).

Fig. 3.17
Good choices
Sugar-free and low-sugar drinks are suitable for those with diabetes.

Sugar substitutes — which ones?

Saccharine, saccharine-based sweeteners, acesulfame K or aspartame can be used by any one with diabetes. Examples of these are the various tablet and liquid sweeteners, such as Hermesetas, Sweetex, Saxin, Natrena, Canderel, etc. (Fig. 3.17). Powder sweeteners, which are mixtures of saccharine and sugar, or saccharine and milk sugar, or saccharine and sorbitol, or fructose (fruit sugar) should not be used without individual advice from your dietitian, but they may be useful in baking or preserve making.

Alcohol

Alcohol need not be avoided, but some care should be exercised.

- Alcohol is a source of a considerable number of calories, which can cause significant weight problems (if you are overweight you should take advice from your doctor).

- Most beers, lagers and ciders are high in carbohydrate and calories. Normally, if you are on a weight-reducing diet, a maximum of one drink per day would be permitted as part of the calorie allowance. It is inadvisable to drink more than an average of three drinks daily on a regular basis and less is preferable.

- Particular care should be taken with beers described as 'low in carbohydrate'. They are not only expensive but have a higher alcohol and calories content than ordinary beers.

- Mixers which contain sugar should be avoided completely (see Table 2). Use 'slimline' varieties.

- Sweet wines are very variable in sugar content and are best avoided.

- Avoid liqueurs.

- Home-made wines and beers are very variable in both sugar and alcohol content.

Remember:

- **Never drink on an empty stomach**

- **Drink moderate quantities only**

- **Never drink and drive.**

TABLET TREATMENT

When to use tablets

When diet alone is not fully successful, then there may be loss of control of your diabetes. In such circumstances tablets may be given in combination with the special diet — tablet treatment is never employed by itself.

Which tablets to use?

Two types of tablets are commonly used to treat non-insulin dependent diabetes, the commoner being those that work by stimulating your pancreas to produce more insulin. These are listed in Table 5.

Occasionally, however, these tablets alone are not completely effective, and in such cases an additional tablet, called metformin (trade name, Glucophage), may also be prescribed. Sometimes metformin may be used on its own.

Remember, too, that you must stick to your diet when taking tablets. You cannot expect the tablets to control your sugar level if you eat what you like — they are not a substitute for diet!

TABLE 5 Tablets used to treat diabetes

Chemical name	Brand name	Chemical name	Brand name
SULPHONYLUREA TYPE			
Acetohexamide	Dimelor	Gliclazide	Diamicron
Chlorpropamide	Diabinese	Glipizide	Glibenese
	Glymese		Minodiab
	Melitase	Gliquidone	Glurenorm
Glibenclamide	Daonil	Glymidine	Gondafon
	Semi-daonil	Tolazamide	Tolanase
	Euglucon	Tolbutamide	Glyconon
	Libanil		Pramidex
	Malix		Rastinon
Glibornuride	Glutril		
BIGUANIDE TYPE			
Metformin	Glucophage		

Some important questions about tablet treatment

Are you at risk until your blood sugar returns to normal?

Initially, your treatment with diet alone, or with a combination of diet and tablets, will take a few weeks to return your blood sugar to a normal level. During this delay, however, you will come to no harm, because the long-term complications of diabetes, which affect the eyes, kidneys and nerves, take many years to develop.

What happens if the tablets do not work?

If your blood sugar remains high, in spite of taking tablets — even perhaps after the addition of metformin — and you are carefully following your diet, your doctor may recommend insulin. In the majority of people, however, this is never necessary. Most instances where diabetes is not brought under control, or where control is not maintained, are due to a failure to follow the diet.

Is there a risk of going into a diabetic coma?

No, this is very rare in your type of diabetes. It never occurs when you are well. If you should become sick, vomit, lose your appetite and become very thirsty and your tests (see Chapter 4, page 59) are positive, you should consult your doctor in order to avoid unnecessary risks.

Can tablets cause side effects?

Side effects are rare. The sulphonylurea tablets cause no ill effects in the many thousands of people who take them. Skin rashes may occur very occasionally. Also, slight swelling of the ankles may be noted in the early stages of treatment, and weight gain of a few pounds can occur.

Some people react with mild stomach discomfort to metformin.

If you are taking chlorpropamide tablets you may develop flushing of the face after drinking alcohol. Although discomforting, it is quite harmless and lasts only a few minutes before disappearing. There is no need to stop drinking alcohol, but if the problem becomes troublesome, a change of tablet might be considered.

Is your treatment effective?

It is clear from the last chapter that the aim of treatment is to return your blood sugar to normal and to maintain it at that level. Unfortunately, how you feel is not a reliable guide to the level of your blood sugar, and symptoms such as thirst, weight loss and passing large amounts of urine appear only if the diabetes is badly out of control. Even with moderately high levels of blood sugar — the sort of levels which can, over a period of years, lead to serious complications — you may have no symptoms. Clearly, some form of test is required which can be repeated at frequent intervals, in order to ensure that your control is being maintained at an acceptable level.

Blood tests v. urine tests

Blood sugar levels can be assessed either directly by means of blood tests, or indirectly by urine tests. Home blood tests are usually unnecessary for those with diabetes not requiring insulin. Urine tests have the important advantage that they are painless. Also, because they are much simpler to perform, they can be carried out easily at home. Therefore for the majority of those with non-insulin dependent diabetes, regular urine testing will provide an effective guide to blood sugar levels.

Urine tests

How urine tests work and their interpretation

When the blood sugar rises, a point is reached at which it starts to leak into the urine. In the majority this will happen whenever the blood sugar is too high, usually above about 10 mmol/l. Therefore, if the blood sugar has exceeded this threshold level since you last passed urine, a test for sugar in the urine will be positive (Fig. 4.1a). If the blood sugar is below this level (normal), the urine tests will be negative (Fig. 4.1b). Therefore, all urine tests, should be negative with your type of diabetes.

Fig. 4.1
How urine tests work.

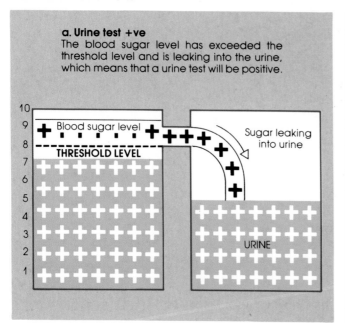

a. Urine test +ve
The blood sugar level has exceeded the threshold level and is leaking into the urine, which means that a urine test will be positive.

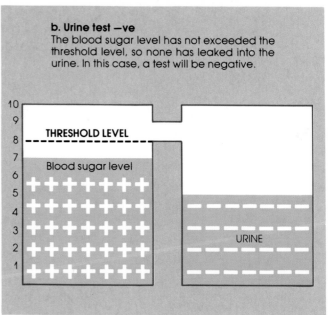

b. Urine test −ve
The blood sugar level has not exceeded the threshold level, so none has leaked into the urine. In this case, a test will be negative.

How often should you test?

To start with, you will be asked to test several times a day, because this will help you to understand what causes the blood sugar to rise. As your urine tests become negative, i.e. as your blood sugar returns to normal, two or three tests a week may be all that are required to reassure you that all remains well.

Stress and illness also increase your blood sugar. Therefore, you would be wise to test your urine several times a day during any illness — even a cold or 'flu' — in order to discover whether your treatment needs to be modified.

When should you test?

Clearly, once treatment has begun to take effect, you will only wish to know if at any time the blood sugar is abnormally high. Therefore,

LUNCH

2 hours

TEST

perform your urine test two hours after a main meal, since it is at this time that your blood sugar will be at its highest.

Keep a record of your tests

Isolated tests of the urine are of little value, but a regular record (Fig. 4.2) gives a much better idea of the level of control being achieved. Such a record will be of particular value when you attend your doctor or clinic for your regular medical check-up. Each test should be recorded on a chart or in a book.

Date / Time	8am	2.30 pm	6pm	10pm	Urine Glucose — Remarks:
Mon	nil				
Tue	nil				
Wed		++			After meal
Thur	nil				
Fri				nil	
Sat					
Sun	+++				Heavy meal night before

Fig. 4.2
Keep a record of your urine test results.

Which urine tests?

Three tests (Fig. 4.3) are commonly available in the United Kingdom:

- **Clinitest,** which involves adding a tablet to urine diluted with water in a test tube, and observing the change in colour.

- **Diastix,** which involves placing a strip of special paper in the stream of urine, and observing the colour change.

- **Diabur-test 5000,** used similarly to Diastix.

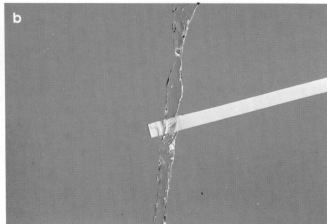

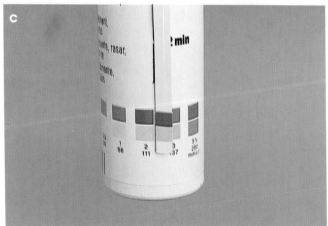

Fig. 4.3
Urine test kits.
a. Clinitest
b. Diastix
c. Diabur-Test 5000

All tests are quite satisfactory. Clinitest is easier to observe, but has the disadvantage of requiring you to collect a sample of urine to put into a tube for testing. Diastix and Diabur-Test 5000, on the other hand, are rather simpler to use, but if your sight is not perfect, may be less accurate.

You will, of course, be shown how to test your urine when you first develop diabetes, but if you have any doubts as to whether you are doing it correctly, check with your doctor or clinic. For reference purposes, full details of the three common tests are provided in Appendix 1, page 91. Remember that urine tests depend on a colour change, so if you cannot see well, or you are colour blind, you may not be able to detect the change and the tests may need to be done for you.

Blood tests

Regular weighing

Factors leading to loss of control

When are blood tests performed?

Blood tests will be carried out when you attend the clinic or visit your doctor, in order to check that your urine tests are providing reliable information about your actual blood picture.

Although you may feel unhappy about handling urine, it is, in most people, perfectly sterile and clean. However, the techniques now available for home blood sugar tests make it possible for you to avoid urine tests if you so wish. Such blood tests require only a single drop of blood, which you can obtain by pricking your finger. It should be stressed, though, that most people with non-insulin dependent diabetes do not need to perform direct measurements of their blood sugar routinely.

Regular weighing is helpful in assessing control. Your weight should not exceed the average weight for your height. Obesity aggravates the long-term effects of diabetes, so if you are overweight you must get your weight down to normal and keep it there.

In certain circumstances diabetes may go out of control unexpectedly. The 5 most common causes of loss of control are:

1. **The development of an acute infection**
   - Urinary infection
   - Large boils, carbuncles or abscesses
   - Severe chest infection
   - More seriously — gastroenteritis associated with vomiting.

2. **After starting certain medications**
   - Especially with steroids (prednisone, cortisone)
   - Sometimes with certain water tablets (diuretics) used in the treatment of blood pressure and heart disease
   - Some tablets and medicines, especially cough syrup, contain a lot of sugar and should be avoided.

3. **Stressful situations**

When people with diabetes are worried or anxious, they may find that their diabetes becomes more difficult to control.

4. **Failure to respond to tablets**

In some people with diabetes, the tablets may lose their effect after a period of satisfactory control. Changing to a different tablet may correct the situation, but a few people may need to be re-stabilized with insulin.

5. **Failure to follow the advised treatment**

Those with diabetes who abandon their diet, stop taking their tablets, or both, will almost certainly become badly controlled, although the deterioration may be quite a gradual process.

In any of these situations, the blood sugar may rise and large amounts of sugar may be passed in the urine. Most illnesses, such as 'flu' and colds, are of short duration and have no significant long-term effects, though the blood sugar, and hence urine tests, may show increases for a day or so. An occasional dietary indiscretion may also show itself in a similar way. If, however, the urine tests become positive for sugar for more than a couple of days, you may need additional treatment and you should contact your doctor.

Vomiting and severe diarrhoea are, however, of greater significance, because they may cause the loss of a substantial amount of fluid and consequently an increased thirst. Although a person with non-insulin dependent diabetes does not develop keto-acidosis (diabetic coma), the salt balance in the blood may become disturbed. If, having taken adequate fluid by mouth, you feel very thirsty and all your tests are positive, you must consult your general practitioner. Very rarely, he may decide you need admission to hospital, so that the large quantity of fluid you have lost can be replaced by intravenous drip, and also because insulin may be required, at least temporarily.

The long-term effects of diabetes and your general health

Treatment of diabetes very rapidly restores health to normal; the symptoms disappear quite quickly, and weight and energy return to normal.

However, after many years of diabetes, some of the body's tissues may be damaged. The eyes, kidneys, and some nerves, mainly those to the feet, are most susceptible. These problems, however, are likely to develop only after many years of poor blood sugar control, and thus occur most frequently in those who pay least attention to their diabetes. Many people with diabetes are completely spared these problems, and even after more than forty years of diabetes, show no trace of any complications.

Foot problems

These are rather more common in your type of diabetes, but can usually be prevented with care. Therefore, this section is particularly important to you.

Damage to the feet

Long-term diabetes sometimes results in nerve damage (called neuritis or neuropathy), which mainly affects the feeling in the feet. The hazard of this condition is that the majority of those in whom it occurs are not aware of the subtle decrease of sensation in their feet.

The feet normally undergo a lot of wear and tear, and any injuries are usually noticed because of discomfort. If, however, discomfort is not felt because of neuritis, increasing damage to the feet may pass unnoticed. In addition, these injuries may be further aggravated by diminished circulation. Ulceration and infection which then occur, can be very serious and result in prolonged periods off work, in bed, or in hospital, and sometimes require operations or even amputations. To a large extent these injuries can, however, be avoided, if proper care is taken of the feet.

63

Therefore, the 'do's' and 'don'ts' of foot care are of great importance, and you should read the following section carefully.

Prevention of foot problems

Scrupulous attention to care of the feet can prevent serious complications. The following measures and precautions are **ESSENTIAL** for **ALL** those with diabetes.

Inspecting your feet

- Inspect your feet regularly — ideally, daily — and if you cannot do this yourself, ask a friend to do it for you. This inspection is important because you may not always be able to feel bruises or sores.
- Seek advice if you develop any cracks or breaks in the skin, any calluses or corns, or your feet are swollen or throbbing. Advice from a State Registered Chiropodist is freely available under the National Health Service.

Washing your feet

- Wash your feet daily in warm water.
- Use a mild type of toilet soap.

- Rinse the skin well after washing. Dry your feet carefully, blotting between the toes with a soft towel.
- Dust with plain talc, wiping off any excess and ensuring that it does not clog between the toes.
- If your skin is too dry, sparingly apply a little cream containing lanolin, or an emulsifying ointment. This should be gently rubbed in after bathing the feet.
- If your skin is too moist, wipe your feet with surgical spirit, especially between the toes. When the spirit has dried, dust the skin with talcum powder or baby powder.

Nail cutting
- When your toenails need cutting, do this after bathing, when the nails are soft and pliable. Do not cut them too short.
- Never cut the corners of your nails too far back at the sides, but allow the cut to follow the natural line of the end of the toe.
- Never use a sharp instrument to clean under your nails or in the nail grooves at the sides of the nails.
- If your toe nails are painful, or if you experience difficulty in cutting them, consult your chiropodist.

Heat and cold
- Be careful to avoid baths which are too hot.
- Do not sit too close to heaters or fires, and protect your legs and feet by covering them with a rug.
- Before getting into bed, remove hot water bottles, unless they are fabric covered. Electric under-blankets should be switched off or unplugged.
- Do not allow wet feet to get cold. Even if they do not feel cold, dry them quickly and put on dry socks, in order to maintain body warmth.
- Do not use hot fomentations or poultices.

Shoes
Shoes must fit properly and provide adequate support. In fact, careful fitting and choice of shoes is probably the most important

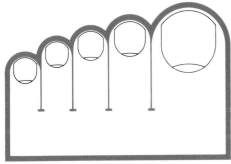

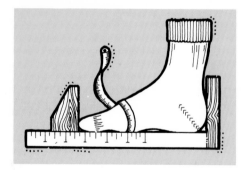

measure you can take to prevent foot problems. Therefore:

- Wear comfortable, good-fitting shoes with soft uppers. Lace-ups with medium heels are ideal.
- Never accept shoes that you feel must be 'broken in'.
- When buying new shoes, always try them on, and rely on the advice of a qualified shoe fitter. Shoes must always be the correct shape for your feet.
- Slippers do not provide adequate support. Therefore, they should be worn only for short periods, and not throughout the day. Do not walk about in bare feet.
- Do not wear garters.

Daily rule: Feel inside your shoes, before putting them on. This is important, because you may not feel nails or pieces of grit under your feet, as a result of lost sensitivity in your feet.

Corns and calluses

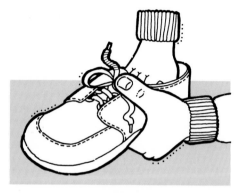

- Do not cut your corns and calluses yourself, or let a well-meaning friend cut them for you.
- Do not use corn paints or corn plasters. They contain acids which can be extremely dangerous to those with diabetes.
- Any corns, calluses, in-growing nails and other foot ailments, should be treated by a State-Registered Chiropodist.

First aid measures

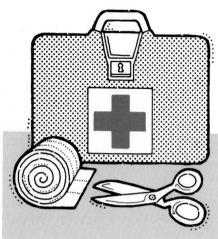

- Minor injuries, such as cuts and abrasions, can be self-treated quite adequately, by gently cleaning the area with soap and water and covering it with a sterile dressing.
- If blisters occur, do not prick them. If they burst, dress them as for a minor cut.
- Never use strong medicaments, such as iodine, Dettol, Germoline or other powerful antiseptics.
- Never place adhesive strapping directly over a wound.
- If you are in the slightest doubt about how to deal with any wound, discolouration, corns, and especially ulcers, consult your doctor.

Damage to the eyes

Two parts of the eye are affected by diabetes:

1. **The lens**

   Opacities in the lens (cataracts) are common in elderly people, and sometimes cause deterioration of vision. Cataracts occur more often in people with diabetes than in normal individuals.

2. **The retina**

   This is the sensitive part of the back of the eye, which is responsible for transmitting visual images to the brain. Diabetes quite often causes minor abnormalities of the retina, without causing deterioration of vision — a condition described by the term 'diabetic retinopathy'. However, in a minority of sufferers, vision deteriorates, and the affected eye becomes blind, usually from bleeding (haemorrhage) within the eye.

Prevention and treatment of eye damage

When cataracts seriously interfere with vision, they may be treated by surgery.

Fortunately, damage to the retina can now be treated and blindness prevented in many instances. Treatment is by laser, a process which involves aiming a fine beam of very bright light at the diseased blood vessels. It is very simple to perform and is often successful, but it has to be undertaken before sight has deteriorated too seriously.

Therefore, it is essential that you should have your eyes tested and the backs of your eyes examined regularly — ideally, annually. This can be done by an optician, by doctors in the clinic, or by an eye specialist.

Some blurring of vision may occur in the first few weeks of treatment, but this is of no consequence and nearly always resolves within a week or two — so don't get your glasses changed. Subsequently, if you should notice a sudden loss of vision in either eye, you must report to your doctor immediately.

```
    A
  O   E
 H L A
N T C O
H L A O T
N T O L A E
L N E T H O A
O T L H E N A C
L H T O C N E A
```

Damage to the kidneys

Damage to the kidneys occurs less frequently than eye damage. Kidney damage must be present for many years before function begins to deteriorate, and even then a few more years usually elapse before the situation becomes serious. Unfortunately, there are no symptoms relating to kidney disease until it is quite advanced. Therefore, regular checks by your doctor are an important means of ensuring early detection of disease.

Painful neuritis

Rarely, neuritis causes pain, usually in the feet and legs, which is particularly disagreeable. A burning sensation, a feeling of pins-and-needles, with an excruciating discomfort on contact with clothes or bedclothes, are the main characteristics of this condition. Unpleasant though these symptoms are, they usually disappear in time, although it may take many months for them to do so. Very good control is an essential part of treatment, and this often requires the use of insulin. Various tablets, including pain-killers, are also used in treating this condition.

Impotence

Sometimes, nerve damage causes impotence. It should be remembered, however, that impotence is also common in those without diabetes. It is often due to psychological causes, and for this reason it is sometimes difficult to discover whether or not it is due to nerve damage resulting from diabetes.

Proper diagnosis is important, and specialist advice should be sought.

Arterial disease

Hardening and narrowing of the arteries are normal consequences of ageing, but with diabetes there may be slight acceleration of this process. Arterial disease can result in heart attacks and cause poor circulation in the feet and legs.

Treatment for these disorders is exactly the same as in those without diabetes. You should take the following precautions:
- Do not smoke
- Do not become overweight

- Have your blood pressure checked annually and treated if necessary
- Reduce the amount of fat in your diet
- Take as much exercise as you can and you will keep the risk of arterial disease to a minimum.

Associated illnesses

Very occasionally, diabetes may be associated with another illness, or it may actually be part of an illness. Sometimes, diabetes develops as a result of the treatment given for other illnesses, such as disorders of the liver and pancreas, excess iron stores in the body, and hormonal problems involving the thyroid and adrenal glands. Generally, such problems will be identified when you first see your doctor, and treatment will be prescribed in parallel with the treatment for your diabetes.

Regular medical check-ups

In the period after your diabetes has been diagnosed, your doctor may wish to see you every few weeks, until he is sure that the treatment is effective. However, when your blood sugar has been brought under control, he may want to see you perhaps every few months or, if you are very well controlled, yearly.

With your urine test records you will be able to keep a routine check on the effectiveness of your treatment. Nonetheless, from time to time it is essential that you visit your doctor or clinic, so that your treatment can be monitored, and any specific problems you might have can be dealt with.

For example:

- Your doctor will want to be sure that your tests are satisfactory. If the record of your tests shows erratic or high sugar levels, he will decide whether additional treatment is necessary.
- He will want to perform a blood test to check your control, because sometimes the urine tests may be misleading.
- He will want to ensure that you understand and are happy with the advice you have been given. This is the time for you to ask questions!
- From time to time, he will want to check whether any long-term complications have developed. It is important that these should be detected before you notice anything wrong, so that early treatment can be commenced.
- Finally, such visits provide you with an opportunity to discuss problems with, for example, your dietitian, as well as reporting any new symptoms, such as difficulty with vision or problems with your feet.

If you are not feeling well, your treatment appears not to be working, or you develop any unusual symptoms, such as worsening eyesight, or abnormal tingling in the hands or feet, report to your doctor at once — **DO NOT WAIT FOR YOUR NEXT APPOINTMENT.**

Fig. 5.1
Regular visits to your clinic are essential.

Summary

It must be stressed that the problems of long-term diabetes occur only in a minority of people with diabetes.

Remember:

- Good control of diabetes often prevents the development of these complications. Therefore, advice from regular clinic attendance is very important.
- Smoking accelerates arterial disease (affecting heart and feet), and may also have a bad effect on your eyes and kidneys.
- Obesity is often associated with arterial disease. Therefore, you should try to control your weight by an approved diet and exercise.

Diabetes and your daily life

Non-insulin dependent diabetes is, in the majority of cases, easily controlled by diet or tablets, and should therefore make very little difference to your daily life. Undoubtedly, the greatest change will be the need to modify and regulate your diet, but other day-to-day activities should be altered very little.

This chapter answers some of the most frequently asked questions about the influence of diabetes in your everyday activities, and discusses topics such as the financial implications of diabetes, and the additional steps you may need to take in order to remain fit and active.

Employment

Diabetes and its influence on your work

For the vast majority of those with non-insulin dependent diabetes, their condition has no effect on their work. Consequently, your ability to function well should be as good as before you developed diabetes, perhaps even better. But there are certain careers in which having diabetes can prove a hindrance:

- If your work involves driving a Public Service Vehicle, and you have to take tablets for the treatment of your diabetes, then certain restrictions may be imposed (see 'Driving', page 77).
- Because of statutory regulations, you will not be allowed to fly aeroplanes.
- In some occupations, employers impose rather strict health regulations. For example, you cannot be accepted for entry into the Police Force, Armed Services or Fire Service, although if you are an established member you should be able to continue without difficulty.
- If you have a potentially highly dangerous job, e.g. deep-sea diving, steeple-jacking, or any job for which very high standards of fitness are required, you will probably have to change your occupation.

Diabetes and your employer

Unless you are employed in one of the occupations mentioned above, your employer need have no fears about your ability to continue employment or commence a new job. Unfortunately, some employers are not aware of the differences between insulin dependent diabetes and non-insulin dependent diabetes, and are therefore often reluctant to employ anybody with diabetes, in the mistaken belief that they might prove to be unreliable employees. Therefore, you should stress to your employer that with uncomplicated diabetes you are as capable of performing your job as a person without diabetes, and without risk to yourself or others. Shift work should pose no problems, and unlike those with insulin dependent diabetes, you do not require specific breaks for snacks or additional meals.

Occasionally, employers will not employ people with diabetes, because of their fear of future problems. In particular, they may be apprehensive that late complications may develop and render an employee incapable of full-time work.

Another frequently encountered problem, but one which usually can be overcome, is difficulty in negotiating superannuation arrangements, on account of the associated life insurance (see 'Life insurance', page 75).

If you experience difficulty in convincing your employer that you are fit to take up a new job, or to continue in your existing one, enlist the help of your GP, hospital doctor or the British Diabetic Association.

Only rarely should a person with diabetes need to be registered as disabled with the Disablement Resettlement Officer at the local Job Centre. However, should you develop serious complications, particularly loss of vision, you may find it helpful to register, and should not consider it a stigma to do so.

Financial implications of having diabetes

Insurance

Having diabetes should not give rise to any serious financial problems. All essential medical requirements are freely available on prescription under the National Health Service. Where you may experience increased expenditure, however, is in the field of life insurance. In all matters relating to insurance, it is essential to be completely frank with brokers or insurers, since concealment of any important medical facts may invalidate the insurance offered, with potentially serious financial and legal consequences.

Motor insurance

If you hold a motor insurance policy you must notify your insurance company or insurance broker that you have diabetes, as failure to do so may cause liability to be denied in the event of a claim. Most insurance companies will continue to offer cover to clients who develop diabetes, on receipt of a satisfactory medical certificate from their doctor. Attempts to impose an additional premium should be resisted.

New applicants for motor insurance may experience problems, but certain companies will quote normal rates, provided no accidents related to diabetes have occurred (there should be none in your case). If you encounter difficulties, details regarding brokers may be obtained from the British Diabetic Association.

Life insurance

Because of the possibility of long-term complications developing, it is normal for some loading to be placed on life and health insurance policies. If your diabetes is perfectly controlled and you have no complications, this loading should be small or non-existent but may be 5-10% on whole life policies. Loading for term assurance, e.g. mortgage protection or endowment policies, will be higher, but will normally be less than for those who are treated with insulin. If you experience any problems, you should seek help from the British Diabetic Association.

Sickness, accident and holiday insurance

It is essential that you declare your diabetes when taking out life or health insurance. Those with diabetes seeking personal sickness and accident insurance are likely to have to pay higher than normal premiums.

Those taking out insurance in connection with travel and holidays abroad must pay particular attention to the exclusion clauses which normally exclude all pre-existing illnesses. However, special cover for people with diabetes can usually be arranged, and the British Diabetic Association can give advice on this matter. Do not forget that failing to declare your diabetes when taking out travel insurance could nullify the policy.

Pensions/superannuation

Your pension rights should be unaffected by your diabetes. If you enter into a new scheme, it is essential that you declare your diabetes.

Other financial considerations

- Prescription charges in the UK are waived for people with diabetes treated with tablets and insulin. A form (CP11) will be signed by your doctor, which will enable you to obtain an exemption certificate. This applies to all prescriptions, whether related to your diabetes or not.
- Your diet should not involve you in any additional expense. If, however, your expenditure has increased and this is creating difficulties, discussion with your local Social Security Office may enable you to obtain some help.
- Those who develop late complications, especially with their eyes, may be eligible for additional benefits.

Driving

Points to remember

You must:

- Tell your insurance company that you have diabetes.
- Tell the licensing authorities (DVLC, Swansea SA99 1AT) that you have diabetes.

Applying for a driving licence

When you apply for a driving licence you have to answer one question of particular importance to you — Question 6(e) asks:

"Have you now or have you ever had: epilepsy or sudden attacks of disabling giddiness or fainting or any mental illness or defect or any other disability which could affect your fitness as a driver either now or in the future?"

To this question you should answer 'Yes' whether you have diabetes treated with insulin, tablets, or diet alone. In the space provided for details, you should state that you have diabetes, adding that your diabetes is controlled by diet/tablets/insulin as appropriate. After you have completed and returned your application form, you may be sent a supplementary form, asking for further information, including the name and address of your doctor or hospital clinic, as well as your consent for the Driver and Vehicle Licensing Centre to approach your doctor for a detailed report on your diabetes. This complication of procedure does not mean that you will be refused a driving licence. The licence will normally be issued for three years and renewals will be made free of charge.

If your diabetes was diagnosed only recently and you already hold a 'life' licence, this will be revoked and replaced with a 'period' licence. Renewals can take several weeks, but should your licence pass its expiry date, you can continue to drive providing you have made application for a renewal.

Heavy Goods Vehicle (HGV) licences and Public Service Vehicle (PSV) licences are not prohibited to those with diabetes who do not take insulin, although some restrictions may be imposed on the Public Service Vehicle driver.

If you have non-insulin dependent diabetes controlled by diet alone, and have normal eyesight (with glasses if necessary), there are no special precautions which you need take. If however, you take tablets, you must ensure that you have your meals regularly, and should not drive if you are already late for a meal.

If you have any problems obtaining a driving licence, you should contact the British Diabetic Association.

Exercise and sport

Exercise is an important aspect of the overall programme to control your diabetes. It not only lowers your blood sugar, but makes the action of insulin on your fat and muscle cells more efficient. Therefore, exercise is very beneficial, and there is no reason why you should not be able to continue heavy manual work or to enjoy any of the sports you played before your diabetes was diagnosed. There are leading tennis and badminton players, golfers, swimmers, cricketers, athletes and professional footballers who have diabetes.

Unlike a person with insulin dependent diabetes, there is no definite need for you to adjust your diet before strenuous exercise. If you are taking tablets, however, your blood sugar may fall lower than usual during exercise, but can be readily put right by an extra snack.

If you are a more sedentary type of person, not given to playing sport, you should, nonetheless, take routine, moderate exercise. Regular walking, for example, is better than short bursts of very strenuous exercise, and it can do much to preserve and even improve the circulation. A great deal of such mild exercise has to be taken to reduce weight, but it can make a contribution towards the general goal of weight control.

Fig. 6.1
Keeping fit is an essential aspect of
maintaining good diabetic control.

Retirement

All retired people have to adjust to the situation created by the cessation of the normal routine of going to work, and the fact that they are no longer associating with colleagues and work-mates. Loss of such contacts and interests may lead to bouts of depression, particularly in those who have never developed hobbies or interests outside their work. However, as long as you are otherwise fit, retirement should cause no greater problems for you than for anybody else.

If you are retired, it is essential that you should not allow your diabetes to stop you from developing new interests, or from making an active contribution to the community. For example, you could undertake voluntary work for the British Diabetic Association or other charitable organisations.

Do not forget to take advantage of the various Social Services available to you. Reduced fares on public transport and reduced entrance fees to certain places of entertainment, for example, could provide you with many opportunities not previously enjoyed.

Maintaining careful control of your diabetes, and taking whatever exercise is possible, are the best ways of ensuring that you remain healthy into old age.

Remember to ask your doctor or dietitian about adjustments to your diet if your activity increases or decreases.

Fig. 6.2
Do not let your diabetes stop you
from enjoying a full and active
retirement.

Travel and holidays

Your form of diabetes should not impose restrictions on travelling or holidays. It is wise, however, to take certain essential precautions, bearing in mind that even people without diabetes frequently suffer unforseen circumstances away from home.

Illness

Mild gastroenteritis is an ailment commonly suffered while travelling abroad, and could cause your diabetes to go out of control temporarily (see 'Factors leading to loss of control', Chapter 4, page 61).

Whenever you feel unwell whilst travelling, test your urine. If the results show a high sugar reading, and you feel very dry and thirsty, consult a doctor. Most of the illnesses you are likely to experience while away from home will be mild and of short duration. Frequently, all you may notice are positive urine tests for a day or so, which then return to normal.

The most important points to remember when travelling at home or abroad are:

- Take your diabetes testing equipment with you.
- If on tablets, take more than you are likely to require. This is particularly important when travelling abroad, in case your return should be delayed.
- When travelling overseas, always take out health insurance.
- Always carry a card indicating that you have diabetes — this is essential if you take tablets.

Fig. 6.3
Always carry some form of identification.

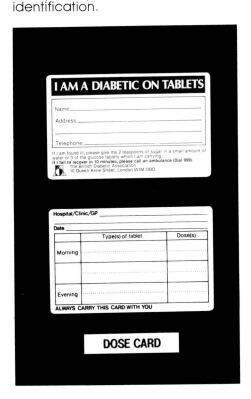

Foreign food

Eating different food, cooked in an unfamiliar way, may cause some problems, especially when eating out. Usually, though, you will find little difficulty in recognizing food similar to that of your normal diet.

An occasional deviation from your normal diet will do no real harm, and may merely cause an isolated positive urine test. If, however, you are overweight and have been on a diet, do not spoil all your prevous good work.

Air travel

You are not subject to any special restrictions, and you need take no special precautions.

Vaccination

Diabetes does not impose any restrictions on the vaccinations you may need if travelling abroad. However, immunization against certain illnesses may be followed by a day or so of feeling mildly unwell, together with a temporary rise in your blood sugar. This should cause you no concern.

Contraception, pregnancy, parenthood

Contraception

Because non-insulin dependent diabetes usually occurs in women who are middle-aged, contraception may not be a matter of concern. If, however, you are of appropriate age, then you should seek advice on contraception from your doctor or family planning clinic. Although the risk to a woman's health from the normal contraceptive pill is very slight, in your case your diabetes may increase this risk slightly. The contraceptive 'pill' may also lead to a rise in blood sugar, in which case some other form of contraception is advisable.

Fig. 6.4
Diabetes should not prevent you
from getting married and having a
family.

Pregnancy

If you are of child-bearing age and you intend having a child, you must take two important precautions:

1. You must ensure that your diabetes is well controlled when you are planning the pregnancy.

2. It is <u>absolutely essential</u> that once you know you are pregnant, you achieve perfect control and maintain it throughout pregnancy. The reason for this is that your growing baby, even though it will not have diabetes, will, nonetheless, be subject to your insulin and blood sugar levels.

Therefore, if you are planning a pregnancy, and certainly as soon as you become pregnant, you must report to your doctor and/or hospital clinic. Also, in order to make sure that your pregnancy continues without problems, you must regularly attend your diabetic clinic.

You may find that you require additional treatment during pregnancy, or even a period in hospital. Such special measures can usually be stopped, however, as soon as you have been delivered. With care by yourself and your doctor, a successful outcome is the rule rather than the exception.

Diabetes and heredity

The question asked by most parents is: "What are the chances of my child having diabetes?" There is no easy answer to this question, because the way in which diabetes is inherited is a complex process, which is not yet fully understood. In non-insulin dependent diabetes it does appear that inheritance plays a more significant role than in insulin dependent diabetes. But it must be stressed that it is most unlikely that any of your children will develop diabetes during childhood, as most inherited diabetes develops only later in life.

Many people who inherit the tendency to develop diabetes never actually do so. This is because other factors, including damage to the pancreas, emotional factors, obesity and, in some instances, even virus infections, are necessary for the development of diabetes.

Diabetes and other illnesses

The effect of illness on diabetes

In the section on treatment (Chapter 4, page 61), it was indicated that under certain circumstances, such as illness or stress, your diabetes may go out of control temporarily. At such times, a few days loss of control is of no real significance, <u>so long as you do not develop symptoms of thirst and dryness of the mouth, or pass large quantities of urine.</u> If, however, these symptoms do occur, you must consult your doctor.

Diabetes and the treatment of other illnesses

Diabetes is no bar to the treatment — including operations — of any other disorder or illness.

With diet and tablets you should be able to control your diabetes. From time to time, however, you may develop problems about which you need specialized advice. On such occasions you may refer to a variety of individuals, including your doctor, nurses, dietitians, chiropodists, the Social Services and, of course, your local hospital clinic.

In spite of the help available to you from these specialist individuals and services, you may well have questions and problems relating to your day-to-day activities, such as careers, insurance, dietary problems etc. This is where the British Diabetic Association can be of great assistance.

The BDA has been working to help diabetics for over 50 years. It provides information and advice on all aspects of diabetes. The BDA also acts as spokesman on your behalf, campaigning for better services and to overcome public ignorance and prejudice. Another function of the Association is to support research to help treat, prevent or cure diabetes and its problems.

The BDA has about 350 branches and groups throughout the UK. They hold regular meetings and social events and can give you support locally. Through your local branch you will be able to meet other people with diabetes which may help you to come to terms with everyday problems of living with diabetes.

The Association depends entirely upon voluntary subscriptions and donations, and needs your support. The more members we have, the greater our influence on your behalf.

Who is available to help?

The British Diabetic Association

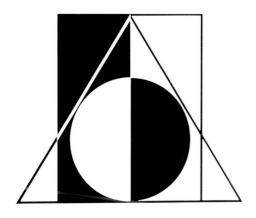

Fig. 6.5
How the B.D.A. helps and supports those with diabetes

Nation-wide organization
In the U.K., there are over 350 local groups, which hold regular meetings — everyone is welcome to attend.

When you have problems
The B.D.A. will provide guidance and help on all problems affecting those with diabetes — but not individual treatment.

'Balance', a bi-monthly magazine
Members receive 'Balance', the magazine of the B.D.A., free of charge, every two months. It reports progress in medical care and the latest news on legislation that affects those with diabetes. There is information on diets and recipes, articles on personalities and practical hints on day-to-day problems.

Holidays and advice for young people with diabetes
The Youth Department runs educational and activity holidays for children and teenagers with diabetes. This gives them the opportunity to learn to cope with their problems whilst taking part in normal activities, without being the 'odd one out'. In addition, family teach-in weekends, parents' meetings and international exchanges are all organized. Pen pals are put in touch with each other. Advice is given on careers and other problems. Photo: Chris Schwarz.

Liaison with Government Departments
The Association maintains close contact with Government Departments and other voluntary organizations, to ensure a mutual exchange of information.

Holidays for adults with diabetes
Summer holidays are organized for adults with diabetes.

Conferences on diabetes
Through the B.D.A.'s Medical and Scientific, Educational and Professional Services Sections, conferences are organized for all people concerned with diabetes, to ensure that they are kept abreast of advances in care and treatment. The B.D.A. is continually striving to make the life of people with diabetes easier and better in every way.

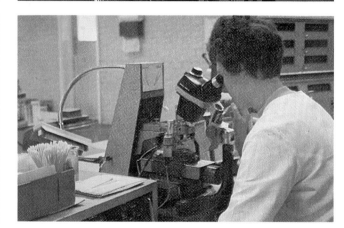

Research
One of the most important aspects of the B.D.A.'s work, certainly the most expensive, is research. The Association is the largest single contributor to diabetic research in the U.K., and currently supports over 60 grants, totalling about £2m.

Some final comments on diabetes and your everyday life

- With relatively straightforward modifications to your daily life, effective control of your blood sugar level is possible.
- Adhere to your diet.
- If you have managed to lose weight, don't put it on again!
- If you need to take tablets, take them regularly.
- Take reasonable care of your general health, and your feet in particular.
- Attend your clinic for regular check-ups.

The late Dr R. D. Lawrence, physician and co-founder of the British Diabetic Association, wrote in his famous book 'The Diabetic Life':

> "There is no reason why a diabetic should not, if he can be taught to do so, lead a long and normal life. True, the diabetic life demands self-control from all its subjects, but it gives in return a full and active existence, with no real privations."

The British Diabetic Association
10 Queen Anne Street
London W1M 0BD
Phone: 01-323 1531
Registered Charity No. 215199

URINE TESTS

There are three reliable tests available in this country — Clinitest, Diastix and Diabur-Test 5000 (Fig. 4.3, page 60). Clinitest is slightly more sensitive and the colour change is easier to observe, but it does have the disadvantage that it requires the collection of a specimen of urine to put in a tube for testing. Diabur-Test 5000 and Diastix have the advantage that they are simpler to use, but if your sight is not perfect they may be less accurate.

There is a fourth test available, Clinistix, but this is not recommended, because it only tells you whether sugar is present or absent.

Urine tests provide a simple method of monitoring your blood sugar level, thereby helping you to maintain good control of your diabetes. When the blood sugar level rises beyond the renal threshold, sugar spills into the urine and will give rise to positive urine test results. Therefore, the aim of your treatment must be to make all your tests negative.

Clinitest

This test (Fig. 4.3a, page 60) requires the addition of urine to a tablet in a test tube and observing the colour change.

Equipment required

This includes:

- A test tube
- A dropper
- A container for urine
- Clinitest tablets.

Directions

1. Collect urine in a clean receptacle.

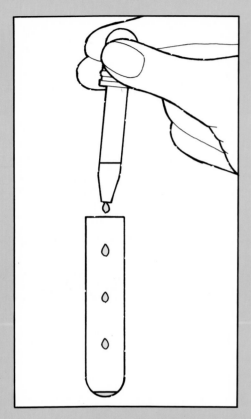

2. Draw urine into the dropper and place 5 drops into the test tube.

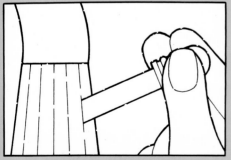

3. Rinse the dropper.

Care and handling of Clinitest Reagent Tablets

● Keep tablets away from direct heat and sunlight (but not in a refrigerator).

● Replace bottle cap immediately after removing the tablet and before starting the test, since the tablets absorb moisture and spoil (turning dark blue) if the bottle is not kept tightly closed.

● Handle tablets cautiously; they contain caustic soda.

Diastix

Diastix (Fig. 4.3b page 60) involves placing a strip of special paper in the stream of urine and then observing the colour change.

Equipment required

This test requires Diastix strips only.

Directions

1. Remove test strip from the bottle and replace the cap promptly and tightly.

   It is important that you:
   ● Do not touch the test area of the strip.
   ● Use only the reagent strips with the pale blue test areas (similar in colour to the 'negative' colour block of the colour chart on the bottle label).
   ● Do not remove the small packet of moisture–absorbing crystals from the bottle.

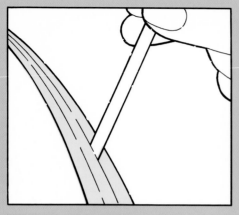

2. Dip the reagent strip into the stream of urine for 2 seconds and remove.

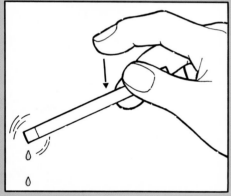

3. Tap the edge of the strip to remove excess urine.

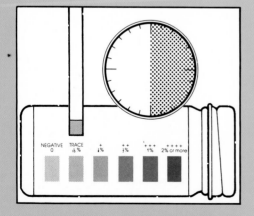

4. Wait 30 seconds and then immediately compare the colour of the test area against the Diastix colour chart, which ranges from 0% (blue) to 2% or more (brown). Record the result.

Note If you are using Keto-Diastix ignore the strips with the buff coloured test area, which are used for the measurement of ketones.

Diabur-Test 5000

The procedure with Diabur-Test 5000 (Fig. 43c, page 60) is similar to that for Diastix.

Equipment required

Diabur-Test 5000 test strips.

Directions

1. Remove a strip from the container.

2. Briefly dip the strip into the stream of urine or specimen.

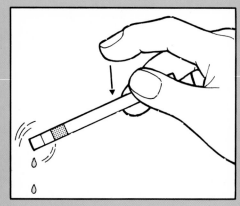

3. Shake off the excess urine.

4. Wait 2 minutes.

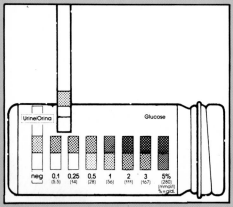

5. Compare the colour of the test area with the Diabur colour scale and record the result.

FOOD VALUES FOR THOSE WITH DIABETES

The first column in the following tables, with the exception of Tables II and VII, lists foods that provide 10 grams of carbohydrate when eaten in the amount stated. The amount is described in either of two ways:

1. A weight measured in grams (g)
2. A spoon measure.

If using the spoon measures, use standard kitchen measuring spoons, as used in compiling this list. The tablespoon (tbsp) measurement is based on a 15ml spoon, the teaspoon (tsp) on a 5ml spoon (all are level spoonsful).

Each item of food, if eaten in the amount stated (either the gram weight or spoon measure), will provide 10 grams of carbohydrate, i.e. 1 'exchange', 1 'portion' or 1 'line'.

For the overweight, the energy (calorie) intake is most important, and therefore the calorie content of each serving of food is given in the third column.

It is generally recommended that at least half of your carbohydrate allowance should come from the foods listed in the tables for starch (Table I) and vegetables (TABLES V and X). Also, the foods marked with an asterisk are all good (*) or very good (* *) sources of fibre, and it is recommended that you include as many of these as possible in your diet each day.

WEIGHTS AND MEASURES

Most diet scales are marked in metric weights, i.e. grams, and we recommend that you use this scale if weighing. If you only have scales marked in imperial weights, i.e. pounds and ounces, the following conversion charts may be useful:

Grams (g)		Approx. ounces
25	=	1
50	=	2
75	=	3
100	=	4
150	=	5
175	=	6
200	=	7

Millilitres (ml)		Approx. pints
75	=	$\frac{1}{8}$
150	=	¼
275	=	½
425	=	¾
550	=	1

TABLE I	Starchy foods
TABLE II	Bread
TABLE III	Breakfast cereals
TABLE IV	Biscuits, crackers, crispbreads
TABLE V	Vegetables
TABLE VI	Fruits
TABLE VII	Vegetables and some fruits
TABLE VIII	Fruit juices
TABLE IX	Processed foods
TABLE X	Milk and milk products
TABLE XI	Low-carbohydrate, high-calorie foods
TABLE XII	Alcoholic drinks

TABLE I

STARCHY FOODS	Approximate measure	Approximate weight of food (g) containing 10g carbohydrate	Calorie content
Arrowroot/custard powder/cornflour	1 tbsp	10	35
Barley, raw	1 tbsp	10	40
Flour, plain, white	1½ tbsp	10	40
Flour, self-raising, white	1½ tbsp	10	45
* Flour, wholemeal, wholewheat	2 tbsp	15	50
** Oats, uncooked	3 tbsp	15	60
Spaghetti, white, uncooked	6 long (19″) strands	10	45
** Spaghetti, wholewheat, uncooked	20 short (10″) strands	15	50
* Spaghetti/macaroni, cooked	2 tbsp	10	45
Rice, white, uncooked	1 tbsp	10	45
** Rice, brown, uncooked	1 tbsp	10	40
Sago/tapioca/semolina, uncooked	2 tsp	10	35
* Soya flour, full fat	14 tbsp	75	300
* Soya flour, low fat	9 tbsp	50	125
* Soya granules, dry	13 tbsp	75	200

* Good fibre content
** Very good fibre content

TABLE II

BREAD	Size of loaf	Type of bread	Approximate weight of carbohydrate (g)	Calorie content
1 thin slice	small	wholemeal*	10	50
1 thin slice	small	white	10	50
1 thin slice	large	wholemeal*	13	69
1 thin slice	large	white	15	75
1 thick slice	large	wholemeal*	20	100
1 thick slice	large	white	26	125
1 roll		wholemeal*	13	69
1 roll		white	15	75

*Good fibre content

TABLE III

BREAKFAST CEREALS	Approximate measure	Approximate weight of food (g) containing 10g carbohydrate	Calorie content
**Allbran	5 tbsp	20	50
**Bran Buds	4 tbsp	20	50
Cornflakes	5 tbsp	10	40
**Muesli (unsweetened)	2 tbsp	15	50
**Muesli (sweetened)	2 tbsp	15	55
**Puffed Wheat	15 tbsp	15	50
Rice Krispies	6 tbsp	10	40
**Shredded Wheat	2/3 of one		80
Special K	8 tbsp	15	50
**Spoonsize Cubs	12-14		45
**Weetabix	1		60
**Weetaflakes	4 tbsp	15	50

**Very good fibre content

Values for all individual breakfast cereals are given in 'Countdown'.

TABLE IV

BISCUITS, CRACKERS, CRISPBREADS	Approximate measure	Approximate weight of food (g) containing 10g carbohydrate	Calorie content
Biscuits, plain	2	15	60
**Biscuits, digestive or wholemeal	1	15	70
Biscuits, cream or chocolate	1	10	60
Crackers, plain	2	15	70
Crispbread	2	15	50

**Good fibre content

Values for individual biscuits are given in 'Countdown'.

TABLE V

VEGETABLES+	Approximate measure	Approximate weight of food (g) containing 10g carbohydrate	Calorie content
**Beans, baked	4 tbsp	75	55
**Beans, broad, boiled	10 tbsp	150	75
**Beans, dried, all types, raw	2 tbsp	20	55
*Beetroot, cooked, whole	2 small	100	45
*Lentils, dry, raw	2 tbsp	20	60
*Onions, raw	1 large	200	45
*Parsnips, raw	1 small	90	45
*Peas, marrow fat or processed	7 tbsp	75	60
*Peas, dried, all types, raw	2 tbsp	20	60
*Plantain, green, raw, peeled	small slice	35	40
*Potatoes, raw	1 small egg-sized	50	45
*Potatoes, boiled	1 small egg-sized	50	40
*Potatoes, chips (weighed when cooked)	4-5 chips	25	65
**Potatoes, jacket (weighed with skin)	1 small-sized	50	45
*Potatoes, mashed	1 small scoop	50	80
*Potatoes, roast	½ medium-sized	40	65
*Sweetcorn, canned or frozen	5 tbsp	60	45
**Sweetcorn, on the cob	½ medium cob	75	60
*Sweet potato, raw, peeled	1 small slice	50	45

* Good fibre content
** Very good fibre content
+ Vegetables which can be eaten freely are listed in TABLE X

TABLE VI

FRUITS+	Approximate measure	Approximate weight of food (g) containing 10g carbohydrate	Calorie content
*Apples, eating, whole	1 medium	110	50
*Apples, cooking, whole	1 medium	125	55
*Apples, stewed without sugar	6 tbsp	125	40
*Apricots, fresh, whole	3 medium	160	40
*Apricots, dried, raw	4 small	25	45
*Bananas, whole	5½" in length	90	40
*Bananas, peeled	3½" in length	50	40
*Bilberries, raw	5 tbsp	75	40
*Blackberries, raw	10 tbsp	150	45
*Blackcurrants, raw	10 tbsp	150	45
*Cherries, fresh, whole	12 tbsp	100	40
*Currants, dried	2 tbsp	15	35
*Damsons, raw, whole	7	120	40
*Dates, fresh, whole	3 medium	50	40
*Dates, dried, without stones	3 small	15	40
*Figs, fresh, whole	1	100	40
*Figs, dried	1	20	45
*Grapes, whole	10 large	75	40
*Grapefruit, whole	1 very large	400	45
*Greengages, fresh, whole	5	90	40
*Guavas, fresh, peeled	1	70	45
*Mango, fresh, whole	⅓ of a large one	100	40

FRUITS+	Approximate measure	Approximate weight of food (g) containing 10g carbohydrate	Calorie content
Melon, all types, weighed with skin	large slice	300	40
*Nectarine, fresh, whole	1	90	40
*Orange, fresh, whole	1 large	150	40
*Pawpaw, fresh, whole	$\frac{1}{6}$ of a large one	80	50
*Peach, fresh, whole	1 large	125	40
*Pears, fresh, whole	1 large	130	40
*Pineapple, fresh, no skin or core	1 thick slice	90	40
*Plums, cooking, fresh, whole	4 medium	180	40
*Plums, dessert, fresh, whole	2 large	110	40
*Pomegranate, fresh, whole	1 small	110	40
*Prunes, dried, without stones	2 large	25	40
*Raisins, dried	2 tbsp	15	35
*Raspberries, fresh	12 tbsp	175	45
*Strawberries, fresh	15 medium	160	40
*Sultanas, dried	2 tbsp	15	40
*Tangerines, fresh, whole	2 large	175	40

* Good fibre content

+ A few fruits contain very little natural sugar and can be taken in generous helpings without counting calories, e.g. cranberries, gooseberries, lemons, loganberries and rhubarb — all other fruits should be counted into your diet.

TABLE VII

VEGETABLES AND SOME FRUITS

The following foods contain no more than 5g of carbohydrate and 20—25 calories in a normal (approximately 100g/ 4oz) serving:

VEGETABLES

*Artichokes, cooked	*Lettuce
*Asparagus, cooked	*Marrow, cooked
*Aubergine, cooked	*Mushrooms, raw
*Beans, fresh runner	Mustard and cress
*Beansprouts, raw	Okra, raw
*Broccoli	*Onions, boiled
**Brussels sprouts	Peppers
**Cabbage, raw	*Pumpkin
**Carrots, cooked	Radishes
*Cauliflower, cooked	Spinach, boiled
**Celery, raw or cooked	*Swede, boiled
*Courgettes	*Tomatoes, raw and canned
*Cucumber	*Turnip
**Leeks, cooked	Watercress

REMEMBER: White sauces count!

FRUITS

Cranberries	Loganberries	Melon
*Currants, red and black	Grapefruit (½)	*Raspberries
Gooseberries	Lemons	Rhubarb

*Good fibre content
**Very good fibre content

TABLE VIII

FRUIT JUICES⁺	Approximate measure	Approximate weight of food (g) containing 10g carbohydrate	Calorie content
Apple juice, unsweetened	6 tbsp	85	40
Blackcurrant, unsweetened	7 tbsp	100	40
Grapefruit, unsweetened	8 tbsp	125	45
Orange, unsweetened	7 tbsp	100	40
Pineapple, unsweetened	6 tbsp	85	40
Tomato, unsweetened	1 large glass	275	50

⁺The carbohydrate value will vary slightly according to the time of year.

TABLE IX

PROCESSED FOODS+	Approximate measure	Approximate weight of food (g) containing 10g carbohydrate	Calorie content
FOODS			
Beefburgers, frozen	3 small	—	450
Canned soup	½ medium tin (thick)	—	170
Fish fingers	2	—	110
Complan	3 tbsp	—	
Ice-cream	1 scoop	—	90
Sausages	2 thick	110	400
Scotch egg	½	—	180
DRINKS			
Beer, draught	½ pint		100
Lager, draught	¾ pint		135
Cider, dry	¾ pint		120
Cider, sweet	½ pint		95
Cider, vintage	¼ pint		75

+ This table lists a few typical foods and drinks which provide approximately 10g of carbohydrate. As there are considerable variations between the products marketed by different manufacturers, it is recommended that if your family uses processed foods regularly, you should refer to the comprehensive lists of manufactured foods and alcoholic drinks provided in 'Countdown'.

TABLE X

MILK AND MILK PRODUCTS	Approximate measure	Approximate weight of food (g) containing 10g carbohydrate	Calorie content
Milk, fresh	1 cup	200	130
Milk, fresh, semi-skimmed	1 cup	200	95
Milk, fresh, skimmed	1 cup	200	70
Milk, dried, whole	8 tsps	25	125
Milk, dried, skimmed	10 tsps	20	70
Milk, evaporated	6 tblsp	90	145
Yoghurt, plain, low fat	1 small carton	150	80

TABLE XI

LOW-CARBOHYDRATE, HIGH-CALORIE FOODS +	Approximate measure	Approximate weight of food (g)	Calorie content
DAIRY PRODUCTS			
Butter/margarine	5 tsp	25	185
Low fat spreads	5 tsp	25	95
Egg — medium uncooked	1	55	80
Cream, single	Small pot	150	320
Cream, double	Small pot	150	670
Cream, whipped	Small pot	150	500
Cheese, Cheddar	Small matchbox size	25	100
Cheese, cottage	5 tbsp	100	110
Cheese, cream	1 heaped tbsp	25	110
Cheese, Edam	Small matchbox size	25	75
Cheese, Parmesan	3 tbsp	25	100
Cheese, Quark	Small pot	100	90
Cheese, Stilton	Small matchbox size	25	115
Cheese spread	3 tbsp	50	140
MEAT			
Bacon, lean, grilled	1 rasher	25	75
Bacon, lean, fried	1 rasher	25	80
Bacon, streaky, grilled	1 rasher	25	105
Bacon, streaky, fried	1 rasher	25	125
Meat, lean, raw	1 av. helping	100	125
Meat, lean, cooked	1 av. helping	100	160
Meat, fatty, raw	1 av. helping	100	410
Poultry, white meat, cooked	1 av. helping	100	140
Poultry, dark meat, cooked	1 av. helping	100	155
Lamb, cutlet, grilled	1 medium	100	250
Pork chop, grilled	1 medium	150	390
Corned beef	2 slices	50	110

LOW-CARBOHYDRATE, HIGH-CALORIE FOODS	Approximate measure	Approximate weight of food (g)	Calorie content
FISH			
Fish fillets, white, raw	1 av. helping	100	80
Fish fillets, oily, raw	1 av. helping	100	230
Shellfish, shelled	1 av. helping	100	80-100
NUTS			
Almonds, shelled	4 tbsp	50	280
Brazil, shelled	14 medium	50	310
Hazelnuts, shelled	6 tbsp	50	190
Coconut, dried	5 tbsp	25	150
Peanuts, roast	1 small packet	25	145
Walnuts	16 halves	50	130
MISCELLANEOUS			
Oil, vegetable	1 tbsp	15	135
Suet, shredded	6 tbsp	50	420

+NOTE: Because the foods and drinks listed in TABLE XI contain a high calorie content, particular care is required if you are overweight.

TABLE XII

The carbohydrate and/or calorie content of a range of alcoholic drinks is listed below. If you are on insulin or large doses of oral hypoglycaemic agents you are reminded **NOT** to exchange alcohol for 'food exchanges' (portions). Providing you do not exceed recommended amount of 3 drinks a day (see page 54) the carbohydrate contribution can be ignored. We do not advise you to drink beers or lager/ciders that exceed an alcohol content of 5%.

Alcoholic drinks		Approximate measure	Carbohydrate (g)	Calorie content
Beer		per ½ pint	10	100/130
Cider, dry		per ½ pint	5	100
sweet		per ½ pint	10	100/120
Lager		per ½ pint	7-10	85/110
Vermouth, dry		1 pub measure (⅓ gill)	1-5	50/60
sweet		1 pub measure (⅓ gill)	5-10	70/80
Sherry, dry		1 pub measure (⅓ gill)	1-2	50/60
sweet		1 pub measure (⅓ gill)	5-10	70/90
Sparkling wine/Champagne	dry	4 fl oz/113ml glass	1-2	80/90
	sweet	4 fl oz/113ml glass	5-10	90/100
Wine (red/white)	dry	4 fl oz/113ml glass	1-2	70/80
	sweet	4 fl oz/113ml glass	5-10	80/100
Spirits, i.e. whisky, gin, rum, vodka, brandy, advocaat		1 pub measure (⅙ gill)	neg	50/70
Liqueurs		1 pub measure (⅙ gill)	5-10	80/100

B.D.A. PUBLICATIONS

Children's books

I HAVE DIABETES

A booklet in the popular Althea series for children and parents which explains diabetes as a story.
Colour illustrations

Diet and recipe books

BETTER COOKERY FOR DIABETICS

by BDA dietitian, Jill Metcalfe. Over 130 delicious and healthy recipes with practical hints for following the low fat, high fibre diet recommended for diabetics. Spiral bound, 16 pages of colour illustrations.

COOKING THE NEW DIABETIC WAY — THE HIGH FIBRE, CALORIE-CONSCIOUS COOKBOOK

compiled by BDA dietitian Jill Metcalfe. Over 260 low fat, reduced calories, high fibre recipes. A useful book for diabetics who need to lose weight. Recipes feature servings for two and four. Eight pages of colour illustrations.

VEGETARIAN ON A DIET

the high fibre, low sugar, low fat, wholefood vegetarian cook book by Margaret Cousins and Jill Metcalfe. An introduction to the benefits of the vegetarian way of eating with specific advice for the diabetic and weight watcher. Featuring a wide range of exciting but practical recipes with an extensive wholefood food values list. All recipes have complete carbohydrate and calorie counts.

COUNTDOWN

A guide to the carbohydrate and calorie content of manufactured foods and drinks.
Designed to help you choose your food wisely.

SIMPLE DIABETIC COOKERY

A booklet of 50 one and two serving high fibre recipes.

SIMPLE HOME BAKING

A booklet of 50 high fibre, reduced fat home baking recipes including cakes, biscuits and breads. The recipes range from basic bread to celebration cakes and all are carbohydrate and calorie calculated.

GLOSSARY

Acidosis
A build-up of acids, usually ketones, in the blood.

Acetone
Is a sweet smelling ketone that may be smelt on the breath of people with ketones in the blood.

Adrenalin
Is the hormone released from the central portion of the adrenal glands in response to a stress or emergency, e.g. an illness, a hypoglycaemic reaction, a fright.

Albumen
A blood protein, which may appear in the urine when the kidneys are damaged.

Beta cells
The cells of the islets of Langerhans in the pancreas that produce insulin.

Calorie
A standard measurement of heat or energy used to assess the energy value of food. It is being replaced by the kilojoule.
1 calorie = 4.2 kilojoules.

Carbohydrate (CHO)
A class of foodstuff that is an important source of energy to the body. It is mainly represented by sugars and starches.

Cataract
An opacity in the lens of the eye that may be caused by long-standing diabetes.

Coma
A state of unconsciousness. In diabetes this can result from severe hypoglycaemia or severe keto-acidosis.

Cortisol

A hormone released from the outer portion of the adrenal glands during stress, shock, infection, etc.

Dehydration

Refers to being depleted of water. It occurs when the blood sugar is high for long periods, as in keto-acidosis.

Dextrose

Simply sugar (see glucose).

Electrolytes

A term applied to the important salts of the body, such as sodium, potassium, chlorides and bicarbonate.

Enuresis

Involuntary passage of urine, bedwetting.

Exchange diet

One in which a fixed number of servings of carbohydrate, fat, protein and milk foods is prescribed so as to control total energy intake as well as the quantities of all major foodstuffs.

Fat atrophy

Disappearance of fat from under the skin, at the site of insulin injection. More common with less refined insulins.

Fat hypertrophy

Swelling of the fat where insulin is being injected.

Fatty acids

These are the main components of body fat in which they are combined with glycerol (glycerine).

Fructose

A sugar occurring in fruit, a simple carbohydrate.

Gangrene

Death of tissue due to poor blood supply.

Glucose

Simple sugar.

Glucagon

A hormone produced by cells of the islets of Langerhans in the pancreas. It tends to raise the blood sugar level.

Gluconeogenesis

The making of glucose by the liver, especially from protein breakdown products.

Glycogen

Is made by the body from glucose and is the main complex CHO in animals. It is stored in the liver and muscles.

Glycogenolysis

The process of releasing glucose from glycogen stored in the liver.

Glycosuria

The presence of sugar in the urine.

Haemoglobin A, (glycosylated haemoglobin)

A test used to assess long-term diabetic control.

Hormone

The name given to a chemical substance released by an organ into the bloodstream. Hormones are responsible for controlling such functions as metabolism, growth, sex development, blood sugar levels, etc.

Hyperglycaemia
A high blood sugar.

Hypoglycaemia or 'hypo'
A low blood sugar (less than 3 mmol/l).

Insulin
A hormone produced by the beta cells in the islets of Langerhans in the pancreas. It enables glucose in the blood to get into the cells and be used for energy or to be stored.

Insulin reaction
Another term for hypoglycaemic reaction.

Intestine
The gut or bowel between the stomach and the anus.

Intravenous glucose
This is glucose that is injected directly into a vein.

Intravenous infusion
Liquid, such as water containing salt and glucose, being slowly injected, usually out of a bottle and over a long period of time, directly into the bloodstream via a vein.

Keto-acidosis or ketosis
A state of overproduction of ketones in the body which causes a build-up of acids in the blood.

Ketones
When fats are broken down in the body, ketones are produced. If a lot of fat is broken down, as in poorly controlled diabetes, the ketones accumulate in the blood, pass into the urine and can be smelt on the breath.

Ketonuria
The presence of ketones in the urine.

Lactose
The sugar found in milk.

Lipolysis
Breakdown of fat caused by starvation or lack of insulin.

Metabolism
The system of chemical control in the body.

Ml
Millilitre, a measure of volume.

mmol/l
Millimole per litre, a measure of the concentration of a substance.

Neuropathy
A disorder of the nerves, where the signals in them are not properly conducted. It is sometimes seen in those with diabetes.

Ophthalmologist
An eye specialist.

Pancreas
A long organ lying across the back of the abdomen. Part of it secretes digestive juices into the intestine, but its islets of Langerhans, pinpoint sized collections of cells scattered throughout it like currants in a cake, secrete insulin and glucagon.

Polydipsia
Excessive thirst.

Polyuria
The passing of large quantities of urine, and in diabetes caused

when there is overflow into the urine of excess glucose from the bloodstream.

Portion

One portion equals 10 grams of carbohydrate in this book.

Portion diet

One in which only the carbohydrate-containing foods are carefully prescribed in quantity in terms of 'portions'.

Post-prandial

After the meal.

Protein

A major food component important in body building, but may provide energy.

Reaction

See hypoglycaemia

Renal threshold

The level of sugar in the blood above which it spills over into the urine.

Retina

The light-receptive layer at the back of the eye. It is an extension of the optic nerve in the eye.

Retinopathy

Damage to the retina. May be caused by long-standing diabetes.

Sorbitol

A sweetening agent which when absorbed is converted in the liver to fructose.

Sucrose

Cane sugar.

Thrush

A fungal infection of nails, skin, mouth or vagina.

Triglyceride

A combination of fats used to carry or store fats in the body.

 Unit

Refers to a quantity chosen as a standard basic measurement of insulin.

 Vitamins

Compounds found in small quantities in natural foods. They are required for normal growth and maintenance of life, although they do not themselves provide energy or substance.

INDEX

Fluids, excess loss of, 19, 62
  see also Drinks
Food
  see also Diet; Meals; Snacks
  basic components, 23-26
  carbohydrate content, 23-24, 28-29,
    38-41
  exchanges, 40, 99-114
  'diabetic', 34, 49
  digestion, 11-12
  effects on blood sugar, 4
  fat content, 24, 30-31
  foreign, 84
  high-sugar, 36-37
  low-carbohydrate, high-calorie, 112-13
  portions, 33
  processed, 110
  protein content, 24, 31
  starchy, 101
  types, 11
    to avoid, 26-27, 36-37
    to eat in regulated amounts, 38-44
    to eat regularly, 46-47
    to eat with caution, 44-45
Fruit, 32, 41-43, 46-47, 106-8
Fruit juice, 109

G

Gastroenteritis, 19, 82
Genital soreness, 18
Glucose see Sugar
Glycogen storage in liver, 12
Glycosuria, 17-18

H

Heredity of diabetes, 6-7, 8, 16, 86
Holidays, 82-83
  for adults, 89
  for children, 88
  insurance, 76
Hyperglycaemia
  causes, 15, 61-62
  effects, 19-20
  symptoms, 17-19

I

Identity card, 82
Illness
  causing diabetes, 7-8, 16
  effect on blood sugar, 62
  effect on diabetes, 9, 69, 86-87
  on holiday, 82-83
    insurance for, 76
Immunization, 84
Impotence, 68
Infection causing loss of control, 61
Insulin
  effect of obesity on, 16
  inadequate production of, 16
  injections, 22
  rise and fall after food, 4, 14-15
  role of, 14-15
Insulin-dependent diabetes
  causes, 6-7
  definition, 5
  people at risk, 7
  symptoms, 9
Insurance, 75
  driving, 75
  holidays, 76
Islets of Langerhans, 3, 13

P

Pancreas, 14
Pancreatic disease causing diabetes, 7
Pasta, 42
Pensions, 76
Pill, The, see Contraceptive pill
Portions see Exchanges
Potatoes, 29
Pregnancy, 85-86
Prescription charges, 76
Processed foods, 110
Protein
   foods containing, 24, 31, 46
   metabolism, 13

R

Rations see Exchanges
Renal threshold of blood sugar, 17, 91
Research into diabetes, 89
Retinal damage, 67
Retirement, 80-81
Rice, wholegrain, 42

S

Seasonings, 47
Shoes, 65-66
Sickness insurance, 76
   see also Illness
Snacks, 34
Social life, 78-84
   eating out, 34, 51-52
   retirement, 80-81
Social Security help, 76
Sports see Exercise
Starchy foods, 101
Stress causing loss of control, 62

Sugar
   blood see Blood sugar
   conversion to energy, 4, 12
   intake control, 22
   in urine see Glycosuria
      testing for see urine tests
   metabolism, 12
   substitutes, 34, 47, 49
Sulphonylurea, 54, 55
Superannuation, 76
Sweeteners, 34, 47, 49
Symptoms
   diabetes, 9
   hyperglycaemia, 17-19

T

Tablets, 22
   lack of response to, 62
   side effects, 56-57
   treatment queries, 55-56
   when to use, 54
   which to use, 54
Thirst, 18, 62
Thrush, 18
Tiredness, 18
Toenail cutting, 65
Travel, 82-84
Travel insurance, 76
Treatment of diabetes, 21-56
   effectiveness of, 57-62

U

Urine
   excess passing of, 17
   sugar in, 17-18

Enrolment Form

British Diabetic Association
10 Queen Anne Street
London W1M 0BD

MEMBERSHIP SUBSCRIPTIONS

Life membership

Single payment of £105 or £15
a year for 7 years under
covenant
£5.00 a year

Annual membership
Pensioner, student on
government grant and
those in receipt of DSS
benefits.

£1.00 a year

Overseas annual membership
Overseas life membership

£10.00 a year
Single payment of £150.00

Please enrol me as a:

☐ Life member: £105
£15 a year for 7 years
under covenant
☐ Annual member: £5.00
☐ Reduced rate
membership: £1.00

☐ Overseas annual member:
£10.00
☐ Overseas Life member:
£150.00
☐ Are you joining on behalf
of a child? (Children in the
UK under the age of 16
can join free for one year if
they wish)

I enclose Remittance/Banker's Order/Covenant for £............................
(Please delete whichever does not apply)

Date.................................... Signature ....

Full name: Mr/Mrs/Miss...
(Block Capitals please)

Address ....

....

Date of Birth.............................. Occupation ....
(This information will be treated as strictly confidential)

The British Diabetic Association (BDA) was formed in 1934 to help all diabetics, to overcome prejudice and ignorance about diabetes, and to raise money for research.

The Association provides practical guidance and information on all aspects of living with diabetes (see page 87).

For over 50 years, the BDA has strived to achieve its aims, but has only been able to move forward with the continued support of its members and supporters. The BDA's authority comes from the size of its membership — the more members, the greater its influence on their behalf.

To become a member, fill in the application form and send it with your subscription to:

The British Diabetic Association
10 Queen Anne Street
London W1M 0BD